Go and Make the Tea, Boy!

Go and Make the Tea, Boy!

Memories of life as a young reporter during the 1960s

John Phillpott

BREWIN BOOKS

BREWIN BOOKS
19 Enfield Ind. Estate,
Redditch,
Worcestershire,
B97 6BY
www.brewinbooks.com

Published by Brewin Books 2020

Reprinted August 2020

© John Phillpott 2020

A CIP catalogue record for this book is available from the British Library.

ISBN: 978-1-85858-711-0

Printed and bound in Great Britain
by 4edge Ltd.

It's yesterday once more...

IMAGINE a time when dinner was 'tea'... when steam trains sent clouds of cotton wool-white billows that cut across the countryside as if some gigantic hidden knife were slowly slicing through a 1950s eiderdown.

Consider, if you can, a pre-motorways twilight when – even on a Saturday – the world and his wife were tucked up well before midnight; an era when it seemed that everyone over the age of 14 years smoked tobacco, the fumes from countless pipes, cigars and cigarettes turning the air bright blue in homes, factories and offices across the land; when men wolf-whistled without shame or censure at women, drank endless pints of mild beer, and wore a collar and tie while digging the vegetable patch.

All this and a thousand other things personified the year that I started full-time employment in July, 1965. And what a different universe from the one in which we live today.

Much of the sexism, racism and ageism that we now rightly condemn were commonplace to such an extent that it might not just go unreported, but invariably allowed to let pass without comment, let alone condemnation.

The workplace was generally a much noisier, a good deal rougher, and a far more argumentative environment than the modern employee would experience, or indeed tolerate, nowadays.

Bullying was often endemic in office, factory, field and farm. This abuse could take the form of unpleasant, aggressive language or rarely – but not entirely unknown – casual violence on rare occasions, despite the universal penalty of instant dismissal for such behaviour.

Yet in many ways, this was a better society than the one we know today. It's true that some men beat their wives and escaped punishment, thanks to the police refusing to intervene in what they euphemistically termed 'domestics'; and child molestation in the home invariably went unreported, being hushed up by the family seemingly with the collusion not only of the perpetrator but also of the wider society.

But there were far fewer murders, no child-grooming gangs in British cities, and acid attacks totally unknown.

1

This was, in many ways, a far more cohesive Britain, a country at ease with itself despite the lingering memory and recent miseries of the Second World War that had been followed by a grey 1950s austerity.

And many people, possibly a majority, were hatched, matched and despatched in the same town or village, leaving the home turf only once a year for the annual two-week works holiday which was invariably spent at the nearest seaside resort accessible by train.

In a pre-internet age, this was the climate in which the local newspaper occupied pride of place in most people's affections. Nearly every home took 'the local rag' and, over the ensuing week, the family might read it cover to cover and back again, before it was reincarnated as combustible material to kindle the household coal fire.

Yes, the culture of home and hearth. How those two went together. And the latter was indeed a focal point in all homes before the Clean Air Acts were brought in to counter the increasingly dense and dangerous urban fogs that were killing hundreds of people across Britain every autumn and winter. Soon, the only casualty would be the open coal fire, which progressively became extinct.

This then was how Britain looked in that far-off year of 1965 when my school days abruptly came to an end and I started work on the *Rugby Advertiser* at number 2, Albert Street…

Tuning in to some heavy metal music

MUSCLES of metal. I gaze at these tireless girders that stretch above me, steel arms embracing this cavern of food, drink and pleasure.

They never weary. Day in day out, year after year, these silent sentinels watch over as ever-changing crowds of visitors, gather and then disperse like myriad shoals of fish fry in the summer river's shallows.

We're sat at a table in one of the many hundreds of chain pubs that have proliferated across Britain over the last few decades. And yes, it's easy to sneer at these halls of cheap pints and a menu heavy with the weight of chipped potatoes.

But come on, this is good, solid grub washed down with chilled, creamy, heavily hop-infused ale. Don't knock it. It fills the gap. You know it does.

But in any event, to mock would be to miss the point… especially so in this particular hostelry, because if the victuals are indeed produced on an industrial scale, then this would only be in keeping with the glorious past of this building.

For my wife and I are in the Rupert Brooke, Rugby, a premises named after the First World War poet who hailed from the Warwickshire town that is arguably the most centrally placed major settlement in England.

The Rupert Brooke, once a print works.

It's no coincidence that the offices of the *Rugby Advertiser* are situated just across the street. And that's because we're sitting in what was the printing factory of the newspaper I knew so well in what seems like a lifetime ago.

Once upon a daydream, this was a factory that rang to the sound of men's raised voices, clattering machinery and the almost ceaseless rattle of teacups perched on tannin-brown streaked trays.

Now it echoes to clinking glasses, the rasp, skid and scrape of knife and fork on plate, and a hundred conversations, melded together to sound like the white noise when a radio dial is caught between stations.

In fact, you could say that it's still a factory of sorts. But instead of ink, oil, newsprint, lead and antimony filling the atmosphere with its dubious perfume, it's the smell of beer and fried food that collides head-on with the senses.

Because back in the time of my youth, when there was a full head of hair to comb, and only a wispy blond down to razor from my top lip, this palace of varieties was almost like a second home for me.

A cliché to be sure, but it does seem like yesterday when I was ferrying messages, hastily scribbled headlines, and late copy to printers with facial expressions that veered from studied disinterest to rank irritation in the time it would take to bellow "Hold the front page!"

Back then, the printers were the industrial elite... and they never missed an opportunity to ram home the point. Famously militant, they guarded the secrets revealed only to them during a seven-year apprenticeship with the zeal of pyramid sentries protecting the doors of a pharaoh's burial chamber.

They spoke a mysterious, technical language that was solely their own, unintelligible to all but the journalists, a lesser species inhabiting the same inky swamp and definitely much lower down the food chain.

I learnt fast. You had to. The main reason why printers had scant regard for their fellow wage slaves was because of the latter's reluctance to take industrial action when required.

It was a chronic flaw in their make-up, you see. *Who do you think you are, mate? Too posh and stuck-up to stick it to the bosses, mate?*

As far as printers were concerned, the only language that the men in suits understood was that of brute force. When push came to shove, the journalists never had any stomach for a fight. *Too concerned with playing the gentleman, that's their trouble...*

And to some extent, they were right. But little did the printers realise that this was the late evening of their lives, they were dinosaurs trapped in warm seas that were soon to evaporate before their very eyes.

For unknown to all, the dawn of the computer age would bring about their mass extinction within just a few, strife-ridden decades. It would be dastardly digital that did for them rather than a comet hurtling into Earth from outer space.

But all that was lying far ahead in the future as this 16-year-old boy carried pieces of paper to and fro between the editorial office and the print factory, and then flee as fast as his legs would carry him back to the relative safety of the reporters' room.

When I entered the world of industry in the mid-60s, most groups of workers were heavily unionised. All things great and small were covered by sets of rules that could not be broken.

To touch any form of printing equipment – be it galley proof, frame or inking stick – was to invite the possibility of a walk-out. So you soon learnt to keep your fingers to yourself, not to push your luck, and basically treat 'the inkies' with a guarded respect even if you didn't actually feel inclined to.

When printers spoke, managements jumped…the latter invariably asking about the height required. An example of this was the milk allowance. Everyone on the shop floor was entitled to a free pint of milk each day, because it was widely believed that milk counteracted the absorption of lead and antimony – the staple components of metal type – that were inevitably lodged in the printer's bloodstream.

Despite the now universally accepted knowledge that these metals cannot be purged from the human body, the practice of free milk persisted right up until the first linotypes were scrapped and the computer keyboards and their companion pulsing display units wheeled in to take their place.

However, there can be little doubt that many printers who had worked in 'hot metal' did indeed go to their graves with lethal amounts of these substances in their bodies.

And the industrial diseases didn't stop there. One that was occasionally to prove fatal was cancer of the scrotum. Printers habitually wore grimy, heavily stained aprons, and because of the height of their work bench or 'stone' as it was called, the middle section of their bodies regularly came into contact with ink and its constituent toxins.

Over a working lifetime, this build-up could lead to a form of cancer that is possibly virtually unknown these days.

Once again, the era of computers would bring about an end to the exposure to these hazards, although quite probably the digital age may yet cause a whole new set of diseases that will afflict workers one day. Perhaps the jury is still out on that one.

But back then, few took an interest in the consequences and prices to be paid in the pursuit of daily toil. There was a job to be done, so it was a question of buckling down, and just getting on with it. The future preoccupation with health and safety was then nothing more than a twinkle in a social reformer's eye.

But who would have thought all those years ago that an entire working world was ultimately doomed to vanish below the waves, like some latter-day Krakatoa engulfed in a final, seismic cataclysm?

So here we are in The Rupert Brooke pub which is not all that far from his actual birthplace in Hillmorton Road, a solid red brick Victorian house of modest dimensions. So please indulge me while I tell of the great man.

Rupert Brooke's birthplace in Hillmorton Road.

The Brooke house speaks of thrift, moderation, commonsense. The building seems to accept its place in the scheme of things, now, as it did then. Very Victorian, it reeks of permanence, a bricks and mortar island set in the turbulent ocean of a changing world.

Despite being sited opposite the overpowering edifice of Rugby School, it has a dignity all of its own.

Brooke was an incurable romantic, unique in the realm of First World War poets. His misty-eyed view of the coming catastrophe of 1914 is in stark contrast to the grim realism of men such as Wilfred Owen and Siegfried Sassoon, two soldier bards who would live long enough to learn that there was no glamour about life and death on the Western Front.

It is fascinating to speculate about Rupert Brooke. There is, of course, nothing new about these sort of posthumous what-ifs. The whole thing goes around in circles. Just look at the number of words expended on Buddy Holly.

People who die young – and especially those who are snuffed out before the full promise of their potential has been realised – are to no small degree blessed by the gods.

It's so easy to speculate. If Rupert Brooke had not been bitten by that mosquito… if he had not contracted that fatal fever… if. Yes, it's all 'ifs'. But even if he had reached the Dardanelles in the spring of 1915, he would probably have been killed or wounded during that ill-fated Gallipoli campaign.

And yes, he might equally have survived, too. But in that case, his poetry would almost certainly have changed course. It is hardly conceivable that the epic line from *The Soldier* – "If I should die", known by millions throughout the world – would have been written post-Dardanelles.

Siegfried Sassoon concentrated on the awfulness of war, as well he might. His time span of survival on the Western Front was nothing short of miraculous. When the life expectancy of an officer was measured in weeks, days even, his continued existence must have seemed charmed.

However, it was this very survival that hardened his attitude to the conduct of the war. The longer it went on, the more a growing revulsion was nourished.

It was down to Sassoon's luck that future generations would form its freeze-frame view of the First World War. The war-is-folly absolute came into being… all officers above the rank of major were murderous lunatics sending the working classes to their deaths. Lions led by donkeys. A flawed myth was born.

The statue of Rupert Brooke in Regent Street.

Wilfred Owen falls somewhere in between Brooke and Sassoon. Whereas the former was talking about "a richer dust concealed", the latter was more concerned with misery, mud and general hopelessness.

The tragedy of Owen is that he almost survived, only to be cut down on the bank of the Sambre Canal just days before the war ended.

The bells that heralded the Armistice were ringing just as Owen's parents were handed the long-dreaded telegram. The great unanswered question is – would Brooke have altered tack had he lived through Gallipoli and gone on to fight in even more murderous campaigns?

One can only guess what would have become of that quintessential young Englishman who is now forever frozen in time, that famous floppy-haired profile gazing into some unseen distance…

Be that as it may, here I am in the pub named after him. I take sips from my beer, anticipating the arrival of my meal. I've allowed myself enough time to daydream about so many things, including the characters I once knew all those years ago.

Men such as Len Tarbox, Harry Duffell, Derek Medlicott… and the kindly Leeson brothers, both of whom had been taught by my father, a teacher at a Rugby primary school.

Once again, I see the expressions on their faces, hear those familiar voices… recall every nuance of countless interactions that were once daily events.

I feel the rough copy paper between my fingers, this hastily scribbled message from Editor Mr Lawson that must be delivered at the throne of one of these lords of all they survey.

Please don't shoot the messenger. I'm just the new boy from editorial. I don't want trouble. Please. Thank you very much. No problem. Oh yes, you had to be very much the diplomat… or pay an as-yet unnamed price.

The meal arrives. I take another sip of beer and tuck into a generous plate of fish, chips and mushy peas. It all seems so appropriate, too.

For this is proper working men's food, without a doubt… and I imagine that the ghosts also sitting around at our table would most certainly agree.

One of the awkward squad, that's me

I ALWAYS thought it was a yawn-inducing cliché when older people talked about how their lives had flown past.

How on Earth could this be, I wondered, as a 20-year-old standing on the cusp of what was undoubtedly an unimaginable span of years that seemed to stretch into infinity before me.

At the age of one score years it appeared that the hoped-for trebling of this number, and then a bit more for good measure, was almost impossible to comprehend, let alone attain.

Yet those older people were of course absolutely correct for I now have the evidence of my own experience. And that's because my half-century-long career in provincial journalism does in fact seem to have flashed by in the proverbial blink of an eye, just like the old folks said it would.

During those 50 years I suppose I must have done all the tasks required on a weekly or daily newspaper, except that of the role of editor. This was a task I turned down on at least two occasions. But why would that be, you may wonder.

My answer to you is simple, for after reading this book, you will almost certainly have gathered the distinct impression that I am what one might term 'a square peg in a round hole'.

The truth of the matter is that during all those days of my working life, I never had much respect or faith in your average newspaper management.

To have been an editor would have put me at the mercy of such people, under their control, abiding by their budgets. No thank you very much. And what if I had to sack someone… or make a mate redundant?

I have known many fine editors in my time and an equal number of duds. But regardless of whether they had real talent or were merely nincompoops in cheap suits, all were obliged to perform such onerous tasks at some stage.

Boardrooms were – and still are in my estimation – invariably made up of time-serving dullards who would rather rise through the ranks of Rotary Club or the Freemasons than develop a cohesive, profitable strategy for their chosen business.

If you consider this to be somewhat harsh, then perhaps bear in mind that these are the self-same individuals who have made thousands of provincial journalists redundant over the last few years.

So my advice to you would be to save your pity for those families who no longer have their breadwinner, thanks to a stroke of the number-cruncher's pen.

Happily for me – either through luck, judgement or a combination of both – I managed to support not only myself but also my family through various and varied journalistic endeavours.

I may not have worked in Fleet Street or roamed the globe as a foreign correspondent. Nevertheless, I have seen sights and experienced adventures that would have eluded most people, so do not feel lacking or deprived in that respect.

For somehow or other, whether by scribbling stories and headlines, or moonlighting as an itinerant pub musician in the evenings, I have held not just body and soul together, but also provided for nearest and dearest, too.

And this is why I'd like to think that whatever lies ahead for me in the future, my life – this far at least – has been reasonably well spent.

So cheers… let's raise a glass to the next half-century, folks!

Len certainly had a head-start in life

LET me tell you about Len Archer. Most of you will be familiar with the long-running television series *Doctor Who.*

Well, it has to be said that he did have a passing resemblance to one of the weird and wonderful aliens encountered by our inter-galactic hero. Now, you may feel that this is a little unfair to our late and slightly lamented chief reporter of the *Rugby Advertiser.*

But the plain fact is that this description of his cranial area is an accurate one. Indeed, I was not the only insolent young hack on the editorial deck to have noticed the strange shape of Len's head.

Narrowed at the chin by an ill-fitting set of false teeth, the collapsed cheeks gradually expanded around the forehead, finally to culminate in the most magnificent St Paul's cathedral dome of a crown.

Stretching across the summit was a heavily greased narrow rivulet of hair combed across from just above the left ear. It clung to the top of his head as if its very existence depended on it, meandering and finally tumbling like a majestic, cascading mountain stream intent on reaching its final destination… just above the right ear.

Those of us who beheld what appeared to be a complete disdain for gravity never ceased to be amazed by this unmoveable entity that yielded to nothing short of hurricane force winds.

Although on one occasion, this heavily oiled slick of a strand did indeed break free from its moorings, to reveal a lariat of hair nearly two feet in length, momentarily reaching for the stars as it hung motionless before once more tumbling back to the glistening pate that was its home.

Len was the supremely competent, highly focused chief reporter on the *Advertiser,* in those days a broadsheet that was published twice a week, on a Tuesday and then in expanded form on Fridays.

The story 'count' was truly immense by today's standards, with anything from 12 to 20 items per page. Nothing escaped Len's beady, porcine eyes… no snippet was too insignificant to merit inclusion in the monochrome expanses of newsprint that was the *Advertiser* in those days.

This was an era when no stone would be left unturned, and Len's charges – a staff of seven or eight reporters – were expected to carefully scrutinise

The Rugby Advertiser offices in Albert Street.

every church or parish magazine, council minutes, court lists, mayor's diary, births, marriages and deaths column with a diligence that perhaps even Sherlock Holmes would have appreciated.

I was the youngest in the reporters' room and once a week was sent out on my rounds, calling at the main post office, railway station, mayor's parlour and parish church in order to gather as much information as possible.

After three or four hours of calls, I would return to the office, my notebook bulging with the day's results. Some would be destined to be inside page doubles, single column stories or occasionally even 'leads', the main story on a page.

The rest would make 'fillers', paragraph-long stories that were handy for filling the gaps when larger pieces fell short.

In those days, page layout demanded that stories were 'dog-legged' with other items lodged 'in the shoulder' of the story immediately above it.

That's right, you have now come into contact with the first technical terms of this book. Welcome to what was once a secret language known only to a select few.

This form of design, broken up with judiciously-placed photographs, meant that it was possible to avoid clashing headlines, something that was then frowned upon.

This style of layout would later be ditched in favour of the 'modular' style, which has remained as the preferred approach with newspapers great and small to this day.

Len was not without humour, but his behaviour at times would these days be regarded as being bullying in nature.

At the age of 16, I was at least five years younger than my colleagues, and so was routinely pushed about by my elders and 'betters'. Len referred to me as 'boy' and this term would invariably be prefaced by a barked command.

He would shout his orders like an Aldershot drill sergeant, rarely saying 'please' and often first announced with a snap of his fingers, a pistol shot that when heard always signalled that a chore was in store.

I would find this irritating in the extreme, but at that stage of my career could not do anything about it, despite my naturally rebellious nature.

At times, it felt like I was little more than his slave, an editorial dogsbody who had no choice but to jump when Len's voice once again boomed across the room.

All his demands had to be met with an unquestioning obedience. In addition to my editorial duties, I had to run not just his errands, but also those of the other reporters.

These were usually to fetch food or take betting slips down to the local turf accountants. And then there was the endless tea making, a beverage that was consumed all day long in prodigious quantities.

It didn't matter what I was doing. When Len bawled "Boy, go and make the tea, I'm spitting feathers," I had to drop everything and leap to attention. When Len told me to jump, I just had to ask how high. That was my lot. The occasional grumble was my only solace.

I started work on the *Rugby Advertiser* on Monday, July 12, 1965. I can clearly recall what I was wearing… a brown, suede jacket, matching trousers, cream shirt, green knitted tie and pigskin shoes with dog tooth serrated soles.

Other than the school uniform that I had unceremoniously abandoned a few weeks earlier, these were the only smart clothes in my wardrobe. My 16th birthday had passed the previous month and I was now very much in the world of work. I had absolutely no idea what to expect.

I was probably aware that I was very young, even by 1960s standards, to be doing such a theoretically responsible job. But with college – never mind university – being very much out of the question, I had very few choices as far as my future was concerned.

I had replaced a reporter called Jim Humphreys, who had recently left for pastures new. He had written a page aimed at young people titled *Teens and Twenties,* dealing mainly with locally-produced pop and rock music, and in particular chronicling the meteoric rise in 'beat' groups that Rugby – along with every town and city across Britain – was currently experiencing.

Rugby had been a village perched on a hill overlooking the Warwickshire River Avon before the arrival of the railways during the 1840s. By the end of the 19th century, it was also a thriving market town, the focus for the agricultural community across a wide surrounding area.

In the early years of the 20th century, light and subsequently heavy engineering arrived in the form of English Electric and, more importantly, British Thomson Houston (BTH).

Rugby gradually expanded to swallow up the neighbouring villages of Bilton, Hillmorton and later on Newbold-upon-Avon. My father had arrived in the 1930s, a job-seeker from Leicester, 20 miles to the north.

He had met my mother while working at the BTH around 1935. They married in May, 1940, and my sister arrived exactly nine months later just as Hitler's blitzkrieg on the Midlands was coming to an end.

A second daughter was born in 1944, but she lived for only a few hours. The doctors then told my mother that for health reasons, she had to avoid having any more children for quite some time. But five years later, I came into the world just before 11am on June 17, 1949, at the Rugby Hospital of St Cross.

After being introduced to the deputy editor – I had of course met the editor at my interview the week before – and sports editor Geoff Ambler, I was shown the tea room and informed that this would be a place I'd soon know rather well.

I was then told that I wouldn't yet be allocated a desk. Instead, I was to take advantage of reporters' absences and sit in their chairs when the need arose. This, by the way, led to constant arguments when returning staff wanted their seats and tables returned to them.

But in the meantime, I was to sit next to a chap by the name of Ted Pincham, who would show me how to rewrite copy sent in by village correspondents, women's institutes and townswomen's guilds.

I quickly got the knack of this and was soon allocated a tiny, cramped space next to Jim Tompkins, a one-legged man in his early 60s who, because of his disability, was confined to the office all day.

He spent much of his time writing up wedding reports that had been submitted as filled-in forms by the happy couple. To avoid the monotony of constant repetition, the introductions – 'intros' as they were called – might begin variously as 'A honeymoon in Blackpool followed the wedding of…' or 'The bride carried a bouquet of stephanotis and lilies of the valley at the wedding of…' or just the plain old 'The wedding took place at Holy Trinity Church, Rugby, of Mr Jack Jones only son of…'

Holy Trinity Church, Rugby.

I can clearly recall seeing my first work in print, an abbreviated village report in which I had faithfully followed Ted Pincham's instructions.

It had the name of the village in bold sans serif type at the top of the piece and the body text would have been something like eight point roman on nine-point leading. This would be my first cutting… and into the newly-bought scrapbook it went.

Many simple and everyday terms such as these were once known only to printers and journalists. Nowadays, thanks to computers, the language of type is universally familiar.

Indeed, I was rapidly picking up the terminology of typography, because in the days of the hot metal print production method, it was very much a journalist's job to work with the printers, appreciate their roles in the creation of a newspaper, and generally develop an all-round understanding of the trade.

One of my duties was to take messages from the editor to the print works over the street. I mainly had to deal with the foreman, Len Tarbox, or occasionally with a genial fellow called Harry Duffell, a dapper little man with a carefully clipped moustache that made him look for all the world like the late great jazz pianist Fats Waller.

But on this occasion, I was given a message by Editor John Lawson to be presented to a bull-necked mound of a man by the name of Derek Medlicott.

I would later realise that he was the proverbial rough diamond, bark worse than his bite, and with a heart of gold. But at the time I was not aware of his softer side. In fact, although I was not scared of him, I always treated him with quite a degree of caution.

So when he read the message, screwed it up, and told me to go back and tell 'Effin' Lawson to stick it up his 'effin posterior' or less polite words to that effect, I was presented with the first major challenge of my fledgling career.

I was in a complete quandary as to what I should do next. Should I tell Mr Lawson that Mr Medlicott had received the message and would reply in due course? Or perhaps I should tell the truth and say that Mr Medlicott had been a bit cross when he saw the message and didn't want to reply at this stage… or maybe say nothing at all?

But one thing was certain. I had to tell Mr Lawson something or I would have been deemed to have failed in my mission, a person not even capable of delivering a simple message and then return with a response.

So with heavy heart, I knocked on Mr Lawson's office door.

"Come in," came the muffled response, a sort of cross between gentlemanly greeting and terse military command.

"Now, Mr Phillpott. What was Mr Medlicott's response to my message?"

Mr Lawson often used a courtesy title whenever he was addressing me, a quirky habit that to my teenage mind seemed a trifle odd.

I had to think fast. "I'm afraid Mr Medlicott seemed displeased and not a little perplexed by your message Mr Lawson," I said, feeling a growing sense of nervousness coming on.

"But what DID he say, John?" Ah, he's calling me by my first name. That's not a good sign. He's becoming annoyed by my prevarication.

"I'm sorry Mr Lawson," I stuttered, "But he used a lot of swear words, language I couldn't possibly repeat in your presence, Mr Lawson."

Mr Lawson abruptly turned on his swivel chair, reddened slightly, and was now hissing his words, telltale danger signs, *"Tell me exactly what he said, boy."*

There was no escape. And I sensed he was not even offering me one, either. I took a deep breath, briefly studied a reflection of myself in the glass of a picture of a long-dead editor of the *Rugby Advertiser,* and said in a tremulous, suddenly high-pitched squeaky voice: "He said 'tell that effing Lawson he can shove his effing message up his effing backside'."

Mr Lawson's piercing blue eyes bore into mine for a moment and then he turned away to gaze out of the window, his stare fixing on to the stream of traffic moving along Church Street.

Without looking at me, he said: "Thank you very much Mr Phillpott. That will be all."

Like a snail, unwillingly to school...

MY mother and father had high hopes for me when I passed the 11-plus and won a place at Rugby's Lawrence Sheriff School in the summer of 1960.

My older sister had recently secured a place at London University, thereby being part of the small percentage of young people who went on to further education in those days.

That summer holiday would be my last few weeks of unburdened, unfettered freedom, although I didn't know it at the time. The weather was glorious, and I spent my days fishing or swimming in the nearby River Swift.

But from time to time, I would catch a glimpse at what awaited me as the sultry days of August melted into early September. Two Churchover boys were already attending 'The Sheriff' as the school was called and occasionally they gave dark hints about what could and often did happen to 'new' boys, such as being 'de-bagged' and having one's trousers hoisted up the school flagpole.

Fortunately, this never happened. It was just their way of teasing me in the ways that 'bigger' boys always have done. Nevertheless, as the fateful day approached, I realised that my relatively carefree existence was soon to abruptly end.

I will always remember that late summer, overcast Monday morning when I stepped for the first time on the asphalt path at the front of the school. Somehow or other, I had managed to cross the busy Clifton Road and reach my destination.

A few weeks earlier, my parents had taken me into Rugby on a 'test run' crash course – no pun intended – on how to cross a road in the town. This had never been an issue in my home village of Churchover because there was hardly any traffic to speak of.

To be sure, one of the family's dogs had been killed after being run over by a bus, but that had been pure bad luck. In fact, Churchover children often played ball games in the street back then. And when it rained, we would dam the gutters to form miniature lakes.

But now I had to be re-educated to cope with the town traffic of 1960. Bearing in mind that the vehicle levels in those days were a fraction of what they are today, this may appear laughable.

But village children in those days just weren't used to all these cars, buses and lorries and the dangers posed by them, which is why my lesson in road sense was vitally necessary.

The first few weeks at the grammar school reduced me to a state of utter confusion. It was some time before I grasped the notion that although room six was the First Form's classroom, quite a number of lessons were conducted in other parts of the school.

I should have realised this when we were told to draw up our timetables, but the plain fact was that either because of confusion or inattention, I often turned up to lessons in the wrong room minus the necessary books.

This caused much amusement among my classmates, but eventually I realised how the whole thing worked.

Mathematics was to remain a complete mystery throughout the five years I was at Lawrence Sheriff. But I soon showed an early promise with history, English and Latin.

Little did I realise back then that my prowess in these subjects would later serve me well when it came to my future career in journalism.

Lawrence Sheriff School.

Science, physics and chemistry would also soon accompany maths into the general fog of confusion, something that might have worried me had I been a bit older and more mature.

But at the age of 12, thoughts of life after school days were over couldn't have been further from my mind.

As I progressed through the school the extent of my skills polarised and contracted even further, with my talent for English and history expanding at the same rate that my aptitude for science subjects was shrinking.

And the school year did go quickly. Or so it seemed. At the end of each term, an overwhelming sense of relief came over me because that meant I could return to my dream world in the village.

Always in the bottom third of the class, my parents had probably given up on me by the end of the third year. But how could I possibly compete with a swot of a sister who never, ever seemed to leave her bedroom, being permanently chained to essays, French and Latin dictionaries and generally feverishly preparing for the next step in what was glittering academic progress.

And that's where the problem lay. If I could never climb such educational mountains, what was the point in anything other than a cursory exploration of the foothills?

Yet there were lighter moments during my time at Lawrence Sheriff, not least of which was the time Queen Elizabeth the Queen Mother visited Rugby and someone in the staff room decided it would be a good idea if the school gave a special welcome to Her Majesty. And so this person devised a cunning plan…

The main suspect was a physical education teacher, a tiny Welshman by the name of Lewis. Naturally, in that lost age – a strange blend of innocence and discipline that we veterans invariably remember through rose-tinted glasses – this five-foot something Celt was christened 'Joe'.

If you have to ask why, then it's obvious you weren't there. Think long-dead boxing legends…

Note that I referred to this man as a 'teacher'. As we happy few, this band of brothers will recall, they weren't called 'teachers' in those days.

No. The word was master.

I can see them still. As one rounded the quadrangle like a man o' war flying every strip of canvas, it was literally a case of Master and Commander, all billowing gowns for sails topped off with a mortar board substituting as crow's nest.

Set the wrong course and you could expect an immediate, devastating broadside. Man the books, you lubbers. Last man up the wallbars will be keel-hauled.

I can see Joe Lewis now. Tiny brown eyes glinting from the centre of a bullet head, sides shaved with a balding Huron-style strip on top. Ex-Army, he had the patience of a sergeant-major with piles and the sensitivity of grizzly bear with its paw in a trap.

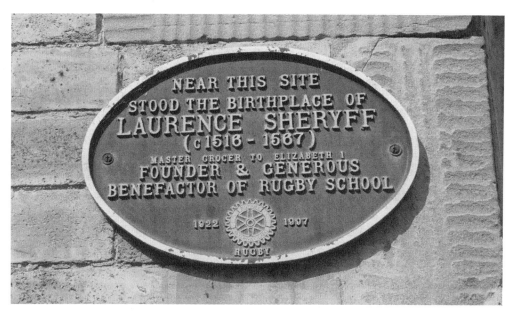

The plaque to the founder of Lawrence Sheriff School.

If you stepped out of line – and that could be anything, ranging from 'dumb insolence' upwards – there was a variety of punishments that increased in severity according to the crime.

The one that sticks in my mind was – as it happens – the wallbars treatment, a form of chastisement that involved racing up and down these vertical wooden ladders until Joe was satisfied that the miscreant was suitably penitent.

Up and down, down and up. "Up again, boy," he would bellow. *"And watch your privates!"*

Thank you, Joe. Your consideration is almost touching. I'm moved to tears. Sometimes literally.

However, Joe Lewis will be forever writ large on my back pages for a wheeze that – had it been successful – might have guaranteed him greater immortality than even his textbook of tortures could bestow.

It was summer at the end of my first year. The Queen Mother was due to visit the town, and scheduled to land by helicopter on the nearby recreation ground. The plan was something so cunningly simple that Joe must have wondered why no one else had thought of it.

Her Majesty was to be given a right royal welcome, as from several thousand feet she would be greeted by the words 'Welcome Queen Mother'…

spelled out in gigantic letters by hundreds of white-shirted schoolboys sitting in perfect order on the school playing fields.

If it came off, what a masterstroke this would be, Joe must have thought. He'd be the star of the staffroom, feted at the school fete, and talked about for years to come.

You never know, someone might even compose a ballad about the whole affair that would be sung in alehouses, old boy association meetings and rowing club socials until the end of time.

Oh, cruel, perfidious fate… how sharp are thy barbs, how thee changeth with the fickleness of the Four Winds.

For it is my sad duty to relate that Joe Lewis' dream of a knighthood was destined to vanish with the speed of a snowflake landing on a Buckingham Palace winter's fire grate.

Oh yes, we practised until perfect. Every boy was instructed to wear a crisp, white shirt, so that the lines making up the characters would stand out against the bright green backdrop of the field.

We were drilled and drilled to form perfect letters… and woe betide the boy who was an inch or two too far to the left or right.

So that precision typographical symmetry was achieved, Joe commandeered what seemed like miles of string to confirm that the words were as near perfect as possible. After all, there was no means of checking.

Hiring a helicopter to page proof, as it were, was not an option.

Those long, hot, days of summer dragged on. Not one passed without a drill halfway during the afternoon… minutes of staying absolutely still in total silence, cross-legged and suffering cramp behind the knees.

"Are you playing Tom Fool, boy? So do you think that Tom Fool is a clever boy? I'll tell you what – Tom Fool is a very silly boy. Isn't he? See me outside the staffroom at four o'clock!"

The wet, sticky heat of June made way for the burning, harsh glare of July. The big day was approaching, and preparations reached fever pitch. Every waking moment seemed to be geared for the great event.

In all honesty, if the Second Coming had been announced during this time, it would have been a toss-up, such was the tumult that took place on a daily basis.

It almost seemed as if such levels of activity had not occurred since the building of the Cheops Pyramid. Like the Great Wall of China, this was a construction that would probably be visible from Outer Space.

Days passed into weeks. The human anthill of living type spilled out of classrooms on a daily basis, countless boys in white shirts and grey, worsted trousers exploding across the summer lawns of Lawrence Sheriff School, molecules of humanity just requiring that vital spark to transform them into those magic words of regal greeting.

This was a well-oiled machine of flesh and blood, now moving to appointed places like automatons, each one knowing his place in the greater scheme of things.

One was reminded of those jellyfish that comprise different organisms, each one playing a vital role, working in symbiosis, the only aim of each tiny component being to bring about the greater good for the whole.

The deadline approached. Joe's mood seemed to vary from crazed martinet to benevolent relative, human being even… ranting when the lines of letters went skew-whiff, beaming with all the warmth of your favourite uncle when things went right.

The day came. With military precision, the jigsaw pieces that would make up this message of welcome were ordered on to the field, roughly 20 minutes before the Queen Mother was due to fly overhead.

Quickly boy, quickly boy. Joe shepherded his young charges, commanded them to sit cross-legged, then ran out his yards of white string. There would be total silence. Upon fear of… well, at the very least, the wallbars treatment.

The seconds became minutes. Still no sound of the helicopter. Time was marching on, and even the stoutest hearts were beginning to doubt. Not a single face dared turn to look at the skies, yet the big question on the lips of these mute hordes was…

Where's that Royal helicopter?

WE must have sat there for three-quarters-of-an-hour when a crestfallen Joe told us to return to our classrooms. Columns of crisp-shirted, but slightly perspiring schoolboys filed back, dejected and downcast.

A few gazed skywards. Not even a seagull, crow or rook dented the azure horizon of this day of ignominy. Not even a swallow doing a low-level strafe for insects. Nothing, ne rien. Zilch.

Eventually we learnt the awful truth. The Queen Mother had landed on the other side of town. A bureaucrat or security man had probably decided that it would be better if she alighted in a different location.

Joe was never the same again. His grand design had foundered on the rocks of circumstance.

Even to this day, I have mixed feelings about my time at Lawrence Sheriff School. The ever-present corporal punishment could at times be savage and over-enthusiastically administered.

Routine humiliation and other forms of mental cruelty was the day-to-day norm. I remember that one boy in my class, unfortunate enough to have a stammer, was mercilessly ridiculed by a master. And bullying among the boys themselves was rife.

But if you survived it, the system could and did produce a small number of boys who went on to become the driven individuals who would take advantage of the coming 1960s, the decade that asked not where you came from but where you were going.

And so, in that summer of 1965, armed with a mere three 'O' levels – the absolute minimum required – I started my first job on a newspaper, one that would go on to lay the foundations of a career destined to last for more than half a century.

Wordsmiths ancient and modern...

AFTER five years of frequently rebellious behaviour at grammar school, fitting in to a new world once again populated by big and little fish wasn't always going to be easy.

A couple of the older reporters often liked to throw their weight around and on one occasion there was even the threat of physical violence. Now, I was a very fit farm boy from rural north Warwickshire and knew how to handle myself, something I made clear when necessary.

This might sound rather extreme, not to say excessive to modern ears, but we are talking about a pre-politically correct universe which the thought police had yet to patrol.

There was a lot of bullying in the workplace in those days and this could break your spirit if you let it. Barked orders for tea and constant demands to run errands – regardless of how much work you were doing – could at times prove to be very wearing.

On one occasion, I refused point-blank to comply with what I regarded as being an unreasonable command. This resulted in a slightly intoxicated reporter saying that he would 'kick my head in'.

In those days, thanks to the labouring work I had only recently relinquished, I was packing quite a lot of muscle beneath my shirt.

Not for the last time during my working life, I invited my abuser to step forward and try his luck. Thankfully, for both parties, my opponent decided that discretion was the better part of valour and backed off.

In many ways, I had just swapped school for the workplace and the environments were not all that dissimilar. It was different jungle, but a jungle all the same.

If Lawrence Sheriff had taught me the basics of survival in life, my four years on the *Rugby Advertiser* were destined to complete my education.

The reporter who I most warmed to was Len Archer's deputy, Guy Edgson. I may have been a bit of a bumpkin but Guy was something else. He was the second cousin of Margaret Thatcher, the woman who would go on to become Britain's first female Prime Minister. His mother was first cousin to the future Iron Lady.

Guy lived with his family in the village of Long Lawford, near Rugby. He was a real old-style character, the like of which has now completely vanished from the modern newspaper office. He sported an enormous mane of sun-bleached hair complete with mutton chop side whiskers, and drove a Bedford van, in the back of which he carried several shotguns, knives and rabbit nets.

When out on his travels, Guy would invariably be accompanied by his pet ferret, just in case he drove past any likely fields or woods and the opportunity to do a bit of rabbiting presented itself.

During working hours, the animal was kept in a box at the back of Guy's van, where it no doubt spent the time having ferret-dreams of future exploits with his hirsute owner.

Once, Guy visited an elderly couple's home to interview them about their impending golden wedding celebration. He thoroughly alarmed the pair by turning up wearing a bandolier of shotgun cartridges and a large hunting knife. And with a ferret waiting in the back of the van, naturally.

The distinctly concerned old couple agreed to be interviewed but nevertheless still rang the *Advertiser* office to check that Guy was indeed a journalist and not a mountain man from the American West or perhaps worse. In fact, I took the phone call and politely informed them that Guy was exactly who he said he was. There was no need to worry.

I always had a special empathy with Guy and that friendship would grow even more thanks to our after-hours guitar sessions in the *Advertiser's* long-disused readers' room.

Around this time I bought a battered old instrument from colleague John Burke-Davies, a reporter who was five years older than me. I quickly learnt the basic primary first position chords, which enabled me not only to play Buddy Holly's entire repertoire, but also any number of folk songs and country music numbers.

Before long, once our night jobs had been written up, that old readers' room would reverberate to the sounds of *Peggy Sue, Every Day, The Sloop John B* and *If I Had a Hammer*.

Reporters could count on at least one night job a week, usually two – and on occasion – a third might be added, especially if there was illness or people on holiday from the office.

And if there was one rule that could not be broken then it was the one that applied to night jobs. Upon pain of a stiff telling-off, all evening work had to be written up as soon as the reporter had returned from the assignment.

Every reporter had to start his or her day with 'empty notebooks', in other words, there was to be no outstanding work to complete in the morning. But once these tasks had been completed, and providing it wasn't then too late, out would come the guitars.

And if there were a few bottles of beer to keep the plectrum fingers greased, then that was all the better.

The trouble was that on a couple of occasions, our zeal for strumming extended into the lunch hour and beyond. More than once the editor burst into the readers' room to tell us in no uncertain manner that it was time to get back to work.

In those days, I played mainly chords. Little did I imagine that one day I would become a reasonably proficient guitarist who would supplement his decidedly unremarkable remuneration by playing in pubs and working men's clubs. But all that was to come about in the next decade.

Not far from Rugby lay the tiny settlement of Cave's Inn, named after the family that had once lived in the area. And at this stage of the proceedings, I'd like to give the reader a little history lesson.

Now, enter any number of newsagents, supermarkets or other stores and the first sight that greets your eyes will probably be the vast array of magazines on offer.

Yes, that broad sweep of primary colours grabs your attention right from the word go. But none of this feast for the eyes would have been possible had it not been for the enterprise and far-sightedness of a north Warwickshire man who can justifiably claim to be the father of modern journalism.

On the boundary between my home village of Churchover and Newton-with-Biggin parishes is Cave's Inn, now a farm, once known as Cave's Hole.

Rugby School.

This belonged to a family of that name and was the birthplace in 1691 of Edward Cave.

He was the son of a cobbler and educated at the original public school in nearby Rugby's market place.

After leaving the classroom behind, Cave was apprenticed to a London printer and at the age of 22 became the manager of the *Norwich Courant*, one of the earliest English newspapers.

For right from the start of his career, Cave was able see the shape of things to come, a talent that would eventually bring him great success. However, the wind-swept wilds of Norfolk were not enough for the young man, and he returned to work in the capital.

Long before the word took on its present – and more notorious meaning – Cave became a 'hack', a jobbing writer who could churn out stories with the regularity of a factory production line. He was soon making a good living.

Cave then got a job with the Post Office, which in those days supplied the emerging provincial papers with London news. Before long, he had made enough money to buy his own printing press, producing pamphlets with intriguing titles such as *A General History of Executions for the Year 1730.*

But his date with destiny came in 1731 with the launch of *The Gentleman's Magazine,* the first of its kind in the English-speaking world. He announced it would be "a monthly collection, to treasure up, as in a magazine, the most remarkable pieces on various subjects of entertainment and matters of publick concern."

It was published from his office in St John's Gate, London, just a short walk from the infamous Grub Street.

Cave's creation was an immediate success. He realised from the start that bulk distribution was the key to high sales – and soon no drawing room in England was complete without a current copy of his publication.

He was also a canny operator, fully understanding the need to exploit contacts, what we would today call 'networking'. And this is where associates from his hack days in the provinces proved invaluable, helping to spread the word.

The Gentleman's Magazine cost sixpence a month and contained essays, debates in Parliament, and reports of bizarre occurrences such as the following:

"Henry Timbrell, a petty farmer near Malmesbury in Wilts, was committed to Salisbury gaol for castrating two lads. He thought to qualify them as (opera) singers and to dispose of them for a good price."

There was presumably a growing market for soprano or falsetto voices in those days.

However, Cave – anticipating the rise of the tabloid press two centuries later – was skilled at keeping his finger on the pulse of the public mood, especially noting a declining interest in politics.

The political essay became less attractive in the 1740s following the Jacobite Rebellion and the growing emergence of provincial papers that would ultimately present a serious challenge.

There was also a clampdown by the authorities when journalists were banned from covering parliamentary debates. But Cave, resourceful as ever, got round this problem by sending members of the public to the House of Commons and then later gleaning information from them.

In another device to get round the law, he also gave politicians the names of eminent Greeks and Romans, or made anagrams of their surnames. Nevertheless, the writing was on the wall for the long-winded parliamentary report, and he started to cut them back, once again anticipating a form of journalism that would one day be known as 'tabloidese'.

Edward Cave died in 1754, after a lifetime devoted to words in an age when most people could neither read nor write. *The Gentleman's Magazine* would prove to be his great legacy, long outlasting him and surviving until the early years of the 20th century. He had been a visionary in the world of early publishing, a prophet who anticipated the boundless – before the advent of computers, at least – future of the printed page.

The development and spread of the printed word was a gradual process. The censorship of printed pamphlets and periodicals in Britain had started to decline during the chaos of the Civil Wars, 1642-51. The conflict saw countless propaganda sheets issued by both Royalists and Parliament.

Many people will have heard of Grub Street, which became an area of London notorious for its scandal sheets and broadsides.

Grub Street took its name from the refuse ditch (grub) that ran alongside. Often ravaged by the plague, it was a haunt of thieves and prostitutes. And the word 'hack' derives from Hackney, originally meaning a horse for hire and later a prostitute. Finally it applied to a writer for hire, a literary mercenary.

A contemporary writer described the hack writer as being feckless, living in a garret and scribbling furiously to earn the next bottle of gin.

Grub Street no longer exists. All that remains of the original street is now covered by the Barbican building.

Journalists regularly covered public executions in the 18th century. Dr Samuel Johnson, wit and compiler of the first English dictionary, reported in great detail the demise of the notorious and sartorially flamboyant highwayman John Rann, otherwise known as 'Sixteen String Jack'.

He was so-named because of his habit of wearing different colour threads to hold up his stockings.

Most provincial papers in the 18th century were politically neutral. There was no point in adopting a partisan stance as this would alienate half the potential readership.

But perhaps Rugby's most famous son was unquestionably Rupert Brooke, about whom I have already spoken, the First World War poet whose premature death in 1915 would famously guarantee his immortality.

But if that aforesaid floppy-haired bard with the faraway eyes did indeed personify an era, what would a certain equally hirsute youth leave behind by way of a legacy exactly half a century later?

The jury's out. And there it will likely remain.

Slings... and Len Archer's arrows

LEN Archer was aged about 35 when I joined the *Rugby Advertiser* but he looked much older.

He was just over twice my age. And yet he might as well been from another century. For a start, if Len was feeling particularly vindictive, he might criticise the clothes I was wearing.

Many people think the 1960s was all about long hair, beads, bangles and purple flared trousers. So it was... to some extent. And it's perfectly true that after work, I might descend on the town kitted out in my finest regalia, a walking Christmas tree of what in retrospect was undoubtedly appalling bad taste.

But as far as work was concerned, I adhered to the dress code. It would be a jacket, worsted trousers, polished shoes, plain shirt and a tie. So what was so wrong with that?

Ah yes, but should this combination occasionally deviate thanks to the usual gear being in the wash – and, horror of horrors – I might be wearing a patterned shirt that didn't meet with the old dome head's approval, then I was fair game.

The trouble was that Len, like so many adults back in 1965, was desperately worried about where all this teenage revolution was leading. En route to his favourite watering hole The London House in Chapel Street, he would often have passed the Il Cadore café where many of Rugby's mods tended to congregate.

This was all rather unfortunate because the Il Cadore was a favourite hangout of mine. On more than one occasion I was obliged to duck below a table when Len passed by en route to the pub.

To Len, teenage culture represented a threat. He would presumably have done National Service and, like so many of the immediate post-war generation, resented the new-found freedom enjoyed by baby boomers such as myself, who he thought had got it far too easy.

It was no mystery. Every time he pulled me up about some sartorial matter, or the alleged length of my hair, some deep-seated frustration was bursting on to the surface.

Once, he asked me whether I'd consider using Brylcreem on my hair. This was yet another transparent attempt to persuade me to conform as by the mid-60s no one over 25 in their right mind used hair cream.

That was for dads and 'straights', people who had quite obviously either shunned or had never heard of The Beatles or Rolling Stones and their penchant for luscious locks hanging free and blowing in the wind.

But of course, these clumsily delivered entreaties made not one jot of difference as far as I was concerned. This was the mid-1960s and things were changing whether people like Len liked it or not.

And what's more, I felt that this was where I belonged… not to some staid and stale yesterday society that reeked of keg beer, cheap aftershave and hair oil that ran down foreheads and stained shirt collars.

But most of all, Len had a problem with rock music and its practitioners. Pop music journalism was in its infancy and provincial newspaper journalists had not quite tuned in to the seismic changes that were starting to shake the Western World to its very foundations.

Newspaper articles in those days came under just a few categories. There were 'off-diary' and 'human interest' stories but the bulk of the coverage would be courts, councils and reports from the umpteen organisations that existed in cities and small towns such as Rugby.

Most pieces would be written at considerable length. And in the case of council reports, councillors were always extensively quoted. This presented a problem, because some of the more self-regarding individuals might make the most of the opportunity to drone on if he or she saw a reporter dutifully writing everything down.

These councillors often looked hard at a reporter as if to say: "I'm a very important person and have something to say. You will take down every word. Would the gentleman of the Press like to start making his notes?"

However, there was an antidote to this, and that involved the reporter visibly placing his or her pen down on the table, folding their arms, and pursing the lips as if to whistle a well-known tune or two.

The best assignments by far were the off-diary pieces, much beloved of chief reporters everywhere, including Len Archer. And the sure way to please him was to follow up something that had been overheard in a pub or other place where people congregated and the resulting tale eventually finding its way into the columns of the *Advertiser*.

Provincial newspapers these days carry very few human interest stories. The few staff still left that have not been made redundant must remain mainly desk-bound in order to produce the sheer volume of copy required.

A major source of extra income was the lineage pool. This was a system whereby stories that were deemed saleable were promptly phoned over to the three main dailies in the region, the *Coventry Evening Telegraph, Leicester Mercury* and *Birmingham Post*.

There was a certain amount of subterfuge involved and stories tended to be sold when the editor was nowhere to be seen, although there's little doubt that he knew about the racket and almost certainly turned a blind eye to the practice.

All the same, there was absolutely no point in anyone pushing their luck. We always used a separate phone located in a little cubicle at one end of the office for sending lineage and I can still recall the number to this day.

So we would dial 100 for the operator and say: "This is Rugby 3280 calling so-and-so and request a transfer charge call." After a few seconds' delay, the operator would get back and confirm that the other party had consented to pay for the call.

You were then put through to a copy typist and dictated your story. To ensure accuracy, the phonetic alphabet was used, for example when spelling a person's name, say 'Bill', it would be 'B' for Bravo, 'I' for India, 'L' for Lima and so on.

Newspapers in those days consumed vast amounts of news, mainly because their circulation areas were so much greater than they are today. Although such a system might appear rather hit and miss, thanks to fast and mainly literate copytakers – almost exclusively endlessly patient women – very few errors occurred.

If there was a major story on 'the patch' it might be worth sending it to one of the national newspapers. Most provincial journalists wrote stories for the 'Nats' in those days.

One of my jobs was to cover Rugby School rugby matches for *The Times*. This was purely because Len had discovered that I'd played the game while at Lawrence Sheriff.

It was very much a case of horses for courses back then. But at the same time, reporters were expected to be capable of covering anything and everything, from village fetes to road crashes, courts and councils to theatre productions.

The statue to William Webb Ellis outside Rugby School.

We even covered auctions, wrote up market reports, and attended dinners but only on the strict understanding that we would be getting fed as well.

In fact, no story was too small or insignificant to merit inclusion in the *Advertiser* columns.

Broadsheet newspapers like the *Rugby Advertiser* had an endless and insatiable appetite for news. One day, during the 1966 General Election campaign, the then Conservative Prime Minister, Sir Alec Douglas-Home visited Rugby.

The sports editor, Geoff Ambler, was a left-winger who had no time for the Tories, and he asked me if I was going to see "Mickey Mouse".

I replied that I had another errand that morning, so probably wouldn't see Sir Alec. Little did I know what would unfold on this memorable day and that there were quite a few surprises in store for me…

That morning, Len Archer fixed me with his gaze, a pair of piggy eyes set in that familiar, fleshy dome of a head.

"Boy," he rasped, "Get on your Noddy bike, pop down to New Bilton, and collect the match reports from Mrs Bradley." These were the Sunday football match reports that had so diligently been collated and collected by this good lady.

Ah yes, the Noddy bike. This was a rather handsome looking Lambretta TV 175, festooned with racks, spotlights and a length of rabbit fur attached to a tank aerial. Well, it was 1966, wasn't it?

Rugby was in a state of great excitement at that time. A General Election was only weeks away, and some political big guns had this north Warwickshire marginal in their sights.

Harold Wilson's gloriously drunken deputy George Brown had already staggered into town, boomed a half-cut speech, and almost assaulted a Rugby School boy who had thrown an egg in his direction.

The Close, Rugby School.

The missile had gone off target and struck an elderly woman. "There – you see! That's why we need a Labour government!" roared George with the dubious logic born of too many Dubonnets. The boy hung his head in crimson-cheeked shame.

It was a sharply chill, sunny morning, so on top of my jacket I wore the mod's uniform of a parka. This, too, sported a rabbit fur collar. For headgear I chose a beret with Union Jack sewn into the crown. No compulsory crash helmets in those days.

Mrs Bradley met me with a mug of steaming coffee. "Cigarette, John?" she wheezed, offering a Kensitas. We settled down to a chinwag in a kitchen that reeked of wet dogs and the mustiness of ancient furniture.

But drinking coffee and smoking cigarettes could only be spun out for so long. I would be missed back at the office. I also feared Len's wrath.

The TV 175's engine sputtered into life and I headed back to base. Turning into Sheep Street, I found myself coming to a halt behind two police motorcyclists. In front was a line of cars, led by a large black and shiny vehicle. I decided to cut down the side and overtake.

This tactic started well, but the lights turned to red and the procession stopped. Then I noticed two more police riders in front. The large car was a limousine and I was now sandwiched between this and the outriders.

The lights changed, and the whole motorcade – including me – moved off. To my amazement, the pavements ahead were thronged with what appeared to be hundreds of waving bystanders. I waved back.

It soon became clear. Turning round, my eyes met with those of Sir Alec Douglas-Home, Prime Minister of Great Britain and Northern Ireland, and top man in the Conservative government, his thousand-year-old aristocratic gaze boring through my skull.

Round the Clocktower we progressed, then past Lloyd's Bank. An old school friend recognised me and pointed, laughing hysterically. Then I saw an escape route.

A quick turn into Gas Street and within seconds I was back in the office. "Where the hell have you been?" raved Len. "We've got to go and cover the Alec Douglas-Home visit."

"Oh yes, I've just met him," I said cheerfully. Len turned on his heel and fixed me with those piggy-blue eyes. "Stupid boy," he muttered under his breath.

There is a delicious absurdity to this sequence of farcical events that could arguably only have happened in the 1960s. This was years before international and home-grown terrorism, when it was entirely possible for the most important person in the land, next to the Monarch, could travel in safety down a public street virtually devoid of security.

It's a long, lost age… without a doubt.

The golden rule of thumb

REGARDING modes of travel, no narrative of the era would be complete without a reference to the noble art of 'thumbing a lift'.

These days, motorists could drive the entire length and breadth of the British Isles and never clap road-wearied eyes on a hitch-hiker. But when I was a young man, cadging a free ride was very much just another form of transport, one that enjoyed equal billing with catching the bus, train, driving a car, riding a bike or motorcycle… or just plain old walking.

This may now seems incredible, but such was the reliability of thumbing lifts as a mode of transport that it was possible to reach any given destination, provided enough time was allotted to the journey.

And, if necessary, it was a method I used as a young reporter – if all else had failed – to either travel to a job or return from it.

Being a lot more relaxed and laid back in my younger days than I am now, the idea of trusting to luck was not as daunting as it might at first seem.

Half a century ago, society was a lot more comfortable in its own skin, far less neurotic and risk-averse, a stark contrast to how it is these days. For a start, there weren't the levels of violence against the individual that there are today.

Admittedly, there is always the danger of the rose-tinted effect distorting one's glasses, but life in the 1960s was, in general, not tainted by the same levels of distrust, suspicion and paranoia that colour so many of our attitudes nowadays.

Like many young people of my generation, I thought nothing of standing by the side of the road at any time of the day or night, and offering my upturned thumb to some complete stranger in the hope of exchanging it for a lift.

Although assignments would ordinarily be reached by more conventional means, occasionally I might cast caution to the four winds and rely on rule-of-thumb.

A number of times, I returned to the *Advertiser* office courtesy of someone I had just met for the first time yet would never ever meet again. However, having said that, being a gentleman of the road was not without its hazards.

On a couple of occasions, I was obliged to open the passenger door at traffic lights or at a road junction and beat a hasty retreat.

And on one unforgettable instance, I leapt from a moving lorry as it slowed down on a sharp bend. Yes, there were dodgy individuals about even in the much glossed-over Swinging Sixties.

But in the main, it was reasonably safe to hitch-hike, sometimes over relatively vast distances.

Two major journeys using this mode of transport that readily spring to mind was a marathon hike from Manchester to Rugby. And another time, a friend and I embarked on a major trek from Great Yarmouth back to the Midlands in the summer of 1967.

The northern odyssey was undoubtedly the most arduous as, on this occasion, the lifts were few and far between, and the time span ranged from early afternoon to the small hours of the next morning.

This was mainly achieved thanks to the generosity and forbearance of lorry drivers, one of whom actually bought me a meal at a service station.

The last lap of this particular journey was by car and took me to Dunchurch, a former coaching village some four miles distant from Rugby. I covered this last stretch at around three in the morning, finally hammering on the door of a work colleague who – in retrospect and most charitably – didn't appear to overly object to his night's sleep being disturbed by some idiot standing on the doorstep.

What never ceases to amaze me, as I view an increasingly misted looking glass, is how youth is endowed with so much seemingly limitless energy, a boundless bounty that can only be fully appreciated peering through the fog of several decades.

Like so many of my compatriots, it was indeed possible to burn the proverbial candle at both ends, yet still perform one's work duties every day. Work hard, play hard. Yes, it's a cliché… yet like all clichés, is based on irrefutable fact.

But whoever said that 'youth was wasted on the young' most surely needs to take that particular saying back to the drawing board for further work.

And so we arrive at the Great Retreat from Caister Campsite in the summer of 1967. And while I would agree that it doesn't have the same significance as the famous retreats from Corunna, Mons or Dunkirk, it nevertheless goes down in the annals as far as I'm concerned.

My friend Bob Ashmore and I had been on a camping holiday, when towards the end of the week, he had all his money stolen from our tent. The cash had been secreted in his black leather coat, and this is what had been taken by the thieves. It's entirely possible that they never discovered the cash.

This disaster meant that we would both be relying on whatever funds I had remaining. I dug into my jeans pockets, and after a quick calculation, figured that there was enough to buy us a couple of huge fried breakfasts in readiness for our 160-mile journey back to Rugby.

So that's exactly what we did. We gorged ourselves until we could hold no more. And then, with rucksacks on backs, Bob and I started walking westwards under an increasingly hot July sun, content at least in the knowledge that the amount of food we had consumed would hopefully keep us going all day.

In all, we had around seven or eight lifts using the patent rule-of-thumb method during the course of the day, and after an eventful 12 hours, we were back on home turf.

On that memorable summer's day we had been given lifts in all manner of vehicles, from a farmer's tractor and trailer to a small lorry. The only time that we thought our luck had either stalled or stopped was when we were dropped off in the centre of Norwich and, for quite some time, failed to get a lift.

Thankfully, we were rescued by a kindly woman school teacher – imagine that today – who burned up a few more miles in a westerly direction on our behalf.

So at last, we found ourselves back in Rugby. And true to form, Bob and I made a beeline for our local, The Raglan Arms in Dunchurch Road, where a couple of pints of beer apiece barely touched the sides.

The following Monday, we were both back at our respective places of work. I have no idea what tasks were given to me that day. But whatever they were, I must surely have devoted some time to daydreaming about our great adventures travelling the highways and byways of what now seems to be a much older, forgotten England... and one that was most surely changing out of all recognition.

Rock and roll is here to stay... I think

YOU will recall from an earlier chapter that I had filled the vacancy caused by Jim Humphrey's departure in the early summer of 1965.

He had written a pop music page that had proved immensely successful, because not only were there many 'beat groups' in Rugby back then, but they also enjoyed a vast number of followers.

There were The Surf Cyders, The Reprobates, The Twilights, Sam Spade and the Gravediggers, The Ravens and The Beat Preachers. And that's just a few of the outfits that played the local church halls, dance halls, youth clubs and pubs every weekend.

But the leaders of the pack were undoubtedly the Liberators – soon to become Pinkerton's Assorted Colours – The Mighty Avengers and, perhaps greatest of all, The Fortunes, who would get to number one in the charts with their *You've Got Your Troubles*.

This song, together with the Byrds' *Mr Tambourine Man* formed the soundtrack to the summer of 1965 and my first weeks of work on the *Advertiser*.

Pinkerton's Assorted Colours went on to chart with *Mirror, Mirror* during the early spring of 1966. This number was written by rhythm guitarist Tony Newman, a Churchover boy and near neighbour of mine.

Tony was very much the local hero – there's a whole chapter devoted to him in my book *Beef Cubes and Burdock: Memories of a 1950s Country Childhood*.

As the decade wore on, some of these groups were destined to achieve global fame, as in the case of The Mighty Avengers who reached number one in the Australian charts with *So Much in Love* written by Mick Jagger and Keith Richards of The Rolling Stones.

Dukes Jetty the title of a number by Pinkerton's Assorted Colours.

So as you can see, the rock revolution of that decade was exceedingly well represented by a certain market town that lies at the very centre of England in its most central county, my beloved Warwickshire.

Jim Humphrey's successor was Dave Berry, not the lead singer of Manchester group The Cruisers, but a rather eccentric young man who had relocated from the north to Hatfield and then subsequently to Rugby.

Dave was barely 21, but dressed and behaved like a character from another age.

He wore ill-fitting, baggy crimplene trousers, and tucked a shirt of dubious hygiene into his underpants. His slightly curly, fair hair was parted at the side with a vague attempt at coiffure that bounced as if attached to a spring on his forehead.

Because he had a tendency to suffer from facial spots, his shaving habits were erratic. And when he did apply razor to stubble, the result was invariably a rather unsightly, bloodied visage dotted with scarlet-stained pieces of paper tissue complete with the last remnants of shaving foam clogging the fringes of his side whiskers.

In fact, he couldn't have been less in keeping with the age. Yet he wrote with a rare eloquence, and especially so when it came to describing the life and times of Rugby's rock and roll fraternity.

And how I envied his role. Occasionally, he would allow me to deputise for him and I leapt at the opportunity. I dreamed of succeeding him, so most Saturday nights would find me down at the Benn Memorial Hall, Rugby's top dance hall.

I met many of the groups that were playing the circuits in those days, including the Artwoods, The Overlanders, Nashville Teens, The Merseys and top Mod outfit The Action.

Back then, the really big acts were still playing provincial dance halls. And with the incredibly easy access afforded to members of the Press such as myself, I made sure that not a single Saturday night was wasted.

One day in the spring of 1967, I discovered that chart toppers The Small Faces were due to appear at the Benn Memorial Hall. The gig was scheduled for a Saturday night – I think it was around April – and I asked Len Archer if I could cover the event and also interview the band.

Predictably, Len gave me his usual disapproving look and said: "As far as I'm concerned, they're just a bunch of long-haired layabouts.

"But if you must, then all right – just make sure you cover the Rugby and District Angling Association annual general meeting at the Peacock Inn first. And no sneaking out early, boy!"

That Saturday evening, I went along to the Peacock, notebook and pencil in hand. And the meeting dragged on and on, members discussing such vital issues as the fall in the gudgeon population on the Oxford Canal or whether to use coloured maggots or not.

And then, finally, it ground to a halt – and I was out the door in a flash, heading straight for the Benn Hall.

I rushed through the doors, flashed my Press card, strode across the dance floor, and within seconds was in the presence of the Small – and, it has to be said – rather spotty Faces.

In those days, I modelled my questioning on the *Melody Maker's* lifelines style of questions and answers, so I asked singer Steve Marriott about his musical influences, favourite food and drink – usually scotch or rum and coke with all the stars – and also requested that he gave me what was essentially a set list of numbers the band was going to play that night. Imagine that these days.

Anyway, they were soon onstage, and were absolutely electrifying. They blasted through *Watcha Gonna Do About It* and Otis Redding's *Shake,* while coasting through the slower soul covers, the titles of which now escape me.

I must have been to hundreds of gigs over the years, but that night at Rugby's Benn Hall was sheer magic, absolutely electrifying. It's more than half a century ago but the cliché still rings true… it could have been yesterday.

Editor Mr Lawson used more of my angling association meeting report in the next week's edition than my Small Faces piece. Ah well, c'est la guerre. But it didn't matter, though. I was meeting the stars, barely two years after leaving Lawrence Sheriff.

On another very memorable occasion I met and interviewed visiting American blues legend John Lee Hooker. By now, I was a well-known figure around Rugby, which pleased me greatly – especially as it improved my standing with the town's young female population.

"Please get me his autograph…" The girls danced around me like whirligig beetles on a summer pond. Please John, <u>DO</u> get his autograph. Me too, said the one in the leather coat, her ocean blue eyes fringed by oil slicks of eye-liner.

It was March 1966. American bluesman John Lee Hooker had been booked to play the Benn Hall, and I was determined to interview the great man. Half-an-hour earlier, I'd flashed my press card and uttered the magic words *Rugby Advertiser* and it was a case of open sesame.

I'd just arrived at the Benn with the pollen dust from Rugby and District Chrysanthemum and Dahlia Society still fresh on my jacket. Today's young hacks are spared such tortures – but back then, major shows had to be covered in depth.

And when we say depth, we're talking journey to the centre of the earth. There would be scores of cup successes and hundreds of classes, winners one, two and three to record.

Get just one name out of place and you'd find out very soon that the wronged exhibitor would invariably be a personal friend of the editor.

But my fledgling rock and roll reporting was rapidly becoming an oasis in a desert of endless shows. Meeting the pop stars of the day when they came to town was a huge bonus.

In this case, it was the massively influential Hooker, ceaselessly cited as being a major influence on any number of 1960s groups, in particular The Rolling Stones, The Who and The Animals.

And me too, as it happened. For I had already fumbled approximations of Hooker's earthy Mississippi Delta guitar sound, with its eerie double-stringing, chord chops, slides and slurs.

The fact that he appeared incapable of confining his muse to the traditional 12-bar format was largely ignored by his many fans, including me. The world accepted his 13-bar blues, warts and all.

By the time I'd got to the hall, there was a local band doing the cannon-fodder slot, wisely omitting such Hooker creations as *I'm in the Mood, Dimples* or *Boom Boom*. Back in the 1960s, such items were beat group staples, along with other workhorses such as Tommy Tucker's *High Heel Sneakers,* Jimmy Reed's *Big Boss Man* and *Louie Louie* by the Kingsmen.

Apart from a scattering of band girlfriends dancing with exaggerated enthusiasm around a pile of patent and fake leather handbags, there was zero interest in these Rolling Stones clones whose name now escapes me.

Meanwhile, the girls in the bar had established a symbiotic relationship with me, mascara-ed remora fish to my reef shark. Yes, yes – I'll get John Lee Hooker's autograph for you all…

Soon it was time to go. I finished my drink, strode through the double doors, and went across a dance floor heavy with the musk of cheap scent, cigarette smoke, rampant hormones and stale sweat.

On the right of the stage was a door marked 'exit' which opened on to a labyrinth of rooms. I headed for the dressing room, and sure enough, there sat the great John Lee Hooker, a slightly-built, coal-black man.

He was talking to a group of young musicians not much older than myself and cradling a cherry-red Epiphone guitar.

"John Lee Hooker, I'm John Phillpott from the *Rugby Advertiser* and I'd like to ask you a few questions please…"

My interview – if you can call it that – was little more than a series of 'lifelines' questions. This was the age when most provincial journalists had no idea what to ask someone as exotic as a visiting American blues singer.

So it was basically a list – favourite food, preferred drink, greatest influences and so on. In a rare flash of intelligence, I asked him to define the blues. *Ain't nothin' but a good man feeling bad...*

His backing musicians flitted around him like courtiers in the presence of a king. They were members of The Machine, a London-based group charged with supporting Hooker on his British tour.

They were attentive but also possessively protective. I felt as if I had entered the gates of some kind of mysterious, forbidden city.

"And now, laydees and gennelmun, we'd like to do one more number before the great John Lee Hooker comes on..."

Right, I'd better wrap it up as the man from Clarksdale, Mississippi, wants to get going. I thanked him, flicked my notebook shut... and then remembered the autographs.

There is one more thing, I said, fingers searching for the list of girls' names I'd hastily scribbled more than an hour ago in the bar. "Would you sign some autographs, please?"

But there was a problem. As Hooker picked up his guitar, a man from The Machine tersely informed me that the girls would have to be disappointed. For as John Lee Hooker can barely read and write, there can be no autographs...

Ah, all right. Perhaps I'll have better luck next week when a group of virtual unknowns will be playing at The Benn. Now, what are they called? Ah yes, the Bee Gees. Or something like that...

Rugby's Benn Hall regularly featured the top groups of the 1960s. The town's proximity to the newly-opened M1 placed it in the middle of the groups' regular touring circuit.

The Kinks, Manfred Mann, The Animals, The Yardbirds and Status Quo all appeared at the hall. The Beatles were due to appear in February, 1963, but never made it. They had become too famous for even a large provincial dance hall such as Rugby's Benn.

In those days, many of these visiting groups would call at nearby Watford Gap services on the M1 for a midnight meal after the show. I readily recall riding on my scooter with other young pop pilgrims from all over Warwickshire flocking to Britain's first motorway services, hoping to catch a glimpse of their idols.

It seemed at one stage that no name band was too big to visit Rugby's Benn Hall. Such as the night that Pink Floyd came to town. And what an eye-opener that proved to be.

This is how I see it, even after all this time, because there are a number of years in the 20th century that will always be remembered by the western world, burned into our collective psyche.

We readily recall 1914, 1939… times of war. Plus the 1912 Titanic disaster, and in 1926, the General Strike. And then there was 1967, the dawn of the legendary Summer of Love.

Pink Floyd came to Rugby Benn Hall probably sometime in the June of that year. By now I had already interviewed The Animals, The Kinks, and John Mayall's Bluesbreakers.

So just who were these Pink Floyd? Pop band, soul… R&B or blues? I decided to find out.

Despite the passage of the years, I still look back in amazement at how easy it was for a newspaper reporter to gain access to all manner of disparate events within the space of a single day. It was perfectly possible to cover a boring old flower show on a Saturday afternoon and mingle with pop stars later that evening. It is an understatement to say that those days are long gone.

The day I met the Pink Floyd was one such as this, the kind of experience we all took for granted then, yet which seems so remarkable when viewed through the mist of all those years.

Down to the hall I went, showed my 'open sesame' piece of card at the desk, and then once again made a beeline for a door on the left next to the stage marked 'exit'. I had now done this so many times.

I walked a few yards down a brightly-lit corridor that smelled of stale cigarettes and sweat, arrived at the dressing room, and knocked on the door. And there was Pink Floyd, sitting having a drink and maybe a smoke or two.

They appeared fairly welcoming, but I have to admit I was not sure about Roger Waters. The thick lips reminded me of Mick Jagger and I was always worried about wise-cracking showbiz people demolishing my somewhat shaky credentials as being a confident and competent man of the Press.

Status Quo had given me a hard time a few weeks before – the lyrics to *Pictures of Matchstick Men* most certainly did not provide any indication as to their lyrical and musical prowess, nor did it hint at what would later transpire as they milked the 12-bar boogie theme for all it was worth.

In fact, they just sat and swore at me. It was all very boring, a bit like the endless walking bass that they were soon to churn out by the lorry load.

So, taking a long draw of the cigarette that was never far from my lips, I latched on to Syd Barrett. He looked the most harmless and possibly the friendliest member of the band.

He had an intelligent and sensitive face, was softly-spoken and genuinely patient enough to answer my cliche-ridden questions. I asked about the music they played, an obvious but necessary query in a media world not quite accustomed to the rock and roll revolution that was now gathering pace.

Around midnight, I returned to the *Rugby Advertiser* office and wrote until dawn, fuelled by a couple of bottles of brown ale and a packet of 20 Bristol tipped. Remember that brand, back in the days when cigarettes could do you little harm and quite possibly were good for your nerves?

I probably produced about a thousand words – far too long – and this was slashed back by Mr Lawson, a man who was rapidly becoming bewildered by the events unfolding during the momentous year of 1967.

Nevertheless, he conceded that I had done a good job and chosen my words with care. My writing style showed promise, despite the fact that I was describing a world that was totally alien to him.

But 1967 was a bit like that – a pivotal year when the new was ushered in and many of the old ways and certainties were soon to wither on the vine.

During the 1960s, many opportunities presented themselves, and I wasn't slow off the mark seizing them by the throat whenever they popped up. Mind you, it wasn't always a case of walking down the street warbling songstress Édith Piaf's *Je ne regrette rien,* I can tell you.

Such as the time when I threw away – or lost – an item of future memorabilia that would almost certainly have boosted my bank account had I decided to sell at some later stage.

It was one summer's morning when the phone went in the reporters' room of the *Advertiser*. Stubbing out the dog-end of my ever-present tipped cigarette into the nearest overflowing ashtray, I picked up the receiver and asked if I could be of assistance.

Those unmistakable Brummie tones droned down the line and my heart almost skipped a beat. "Hallo mate, are you a reporter? This is Carl Wayne of the Move and I've got a story for you. I'm in a phone box and my pennies are running out – could you ring me back?"

My hand was probably shaking slightly as I scribbled down the number of whatever Birmingham red phone box the Midlands pop star was calling from.

And as I replaced the black Bakelite phone, I remember a momentary flash of doubt over whether I'd heard him properly and got the number wrong.

Paranoid? Oh no, that would be a future Black Sabbath theme of a few years later.

Anyway, the gist of it was this. The Move had commissioned a cartoonist to illustrate a postcard to publicise the band's forthcoming release of a single titled *Flowers in the Rain*.

So if they sent me some information, a few publicity shots plus the postcard, would I write a piece for the *Rugby Advertiser*? Hmmm…hey, what do bears do in the woods, eh?

A couple of days later, a publicity pack duly arrived and there was the postcard, which depicted a naked Prime Minister Harold Wilson together with broad hints that his private life might not be all it seemed.

This was the man who was then busy shutting down the pirate radio stations as part of his Labour government's war on 'psychedelic anarchists' and it wasn't long before he set in motion a legal action against the Move, threatening all manner of retribution if the postcard wasn't withdrawn immediately.

In the end, the Move caved into the old schemer's bullying and agreed to pay the record's royalties to charities of Wilson's choice.

But in the meantime, I'd lost my personal copy of the postcard… and even more than half a century later after that fateful day in 1967 when Carl Wayne got on the blower, I still occasionally daydream about the money I might have made if this morsel of Sixties memorabilia had been sold to a collector.

But now we come to the best of all, this time to the summer bank holiday of 1967, when the late great Jimi Hendrix appeared at Woburn Abbey in Buckinghamshire.

I was with a friend supping a jar or two down at the Raglan Arms in Dunchurch Road, and we were debating how to spend these glorious three days of freedom.

Let's go and see the ace axeman suggested my pal… and so, without further ado, Chris James and I rang our respective parents to say that we would be away for a while.

My Lambretta TV 175 was soon heading down the M1 to Woburn, its two-stroke engine popping and purring away those miles in a heady slipstream of light blue smoke.

With the wind in our hair – yes, I actually had some back then and crash helmets had not yet become a legal requirement – we arrived at a wood near the festival site where we spent a cold night curled up under the trees and hoping to get some sleep before the rock and roll cranked up.

I seem to recall that I spent most of that night watching shooting stars and listening to the hoot of owls in that late summer woodland rather than sleeping... but it didn't matter.

Because the next day – when we emerged blinking into bright sunlight as dawn rose above Britain's first real pop festival – we somehow knew that the great man would soon be squeezing his Fender Stratocaster until it pleaded for mercy... and rock music would never be the same again.

Mind you, it didn't always go well for me. On one occasion I covered a 'flower power' gig at Webb Ellis Road rugby ground clubhouse. Top Rugby band Jigsaw – they were called 'bands' now – were playing the gig, supported by The Big Idea, now reincarnated from the remnants of The Reprobates.

Sadly, the actual flowers were few and far between, and what blooms existed were soon to wither and die, either in the heat of the night, or because they'd been trodden on by dancers.

Jigsaw was one of the area's top outfits and up and until then I'd always praised them in print. But this didn't stop them rounding on me the next week after my report had appeared in the *Advertiser.*

It's perfectly true that I had written a slightly satirical, tongue-in-cheek piece, but the band members took great offence at this and cornered me outside the clubhouse.

One of the band, bass player Barrie Bernard, even went a step further and later added injury to insult by haranguing me over the microphone continuously throughout the evening.

But nobly defended by my friend Brian Meredith, drummer with The Big Idea, I weathered the storm to live and write another day.

However, by that stage, I was afraid of nothing and feared no one. I had a natural rebellious streak and refused to be intimidated by anything or anybody.

I was only 18 years old, but had seen a lot of life in my first two years on the *Advertiser,* met all manner of people from mayors and rock stars to labourers, and knew instinctively how to behave and react in any given situation.

An exchange of words outside a ramshackle wooden hut on a summer's evening was small beer, to say the least.

And then it happened. Dave Berry handed in his notice. He had got a job on the *Lancashire Evening Post* and the editor told me that the pop page was mine if I wanted it. My dream had come true at last.

The times they were a'changing

JUST because I was now the pop music editor of the *Rugby Advertiser* didn't mean that I was excused all other duties.

It's a long time ago now but I seem to recall that I was allowed about a day-and-a-half to unearth and write enough stories to fill a wide open, advertisement-free broadsheet page.

Whenever I hadn't been assigned a regular night job, such as Braunston Parish Council just over the border in neighbouring Northamptonshire, I would be out and about writing play reviews, interviewing local rock groups and covering folk music gigs.

The latter often featured big names, regulars on the British folk circuit that was then flourishing and attracting all sorts of people, not just the diehard fans.

I can recall seeing Derek Brimstone, Vin Garbutt and also interviewing Scottish singer and guitarist Alex Campbell, a man with a serious whisky habit that quite possibly would cause his eventual downfall.

And John Martyn came to town once and was beginning to adopt the percussive, avant garde and impressionistic guitar style infused with Eastern mysticism that would ultimately lead to his later global cross-over success.

By this time, Len Archer had probably grudgingly come to understand that the future readers of the *Rugby Advertiser* were today's youngsters and the paper had to reflect this fact.

Even so, as I tapped away on my ancient Remington typewriter during my 'pop page day,' I would be aware of his beady blue eyes drilling into my back, ever watchful for a moment's lull in the proceedings that might offer him an opportunity to have what he jokingly and slightly mischievously called 'a welcome break.'

Of course, this was actually nothing of the sort, and usually meant me being obliged to drop everything to harvest a few stories from some council minutes or to see a person who had called into the front office.

Thankfully, he left me alone most of the time. He may not have understood much of what I was writing – and liked its subjects even less – but the editor obviously felt it was important and this reality was probably slowly dawning on Len.

But one morning, Len and sports editor Geoff Ambler were having a conversation about the previous night's televised performance at the London Palladium by The Rolling Stones.

They both agreed that the band's refusal to join the other acts on the famous revolving stage was a pretty heinous crime. Absolutely disgusting, they huffed and puffed.

The Stones had played *Let's Spend the Night Together* – which was bad enough – but what really bothered them was the sight of guitarist and piano player Brian Jones, a vision of debauched androgyny and mid-60s decadence.

It wasn't long before I got the loaded question treatment. *And what did young John think about the show?*

My reply naturally confirmed their worst suspicions. Len's attitude was no surprise, but Geoff Ambler's dismissal of the band disappointed me because he made no secret of the fact that he was an avowed left-winger who always portrayed himself as being a man of the people.

He wrote a weekly column titled *Around the Clocktower* but it was not long before this was stopped by the editor because of its socialist bias. This was plainly wrong. In those days, it was the nasty old Tories who disliked the concept of free speech, unlike nowadays when the boot is most firmly on the left foot.

I hadn't realised this at the time, but had yet to learn that bigotry and the urge to silence dissent was not the prerogative of any particular political party or persuasion.

In my naivety, I assumed that being on the Left meant you were basically anti-establishment, and would therefore theoretically approve of The Stones' mildly anarchic gestures.

But no. Geoff Ambler was just the same as all the other uptight adults who couldn't understand that society was changing.

But perhaps I should have known, for a few weeks earlier, a pair of long-haired young men had called at the front office. I was sent down to speak to them and was intrigued to learn that they were in the process of setting up a Campaign for Nuclear Disarmament (CND) branch in Rugby.

I filled several pages of my notebook with what they had to say but was bitterly disappointed when Geoff Ambler dismissed them as 'long-haired layabouts' and told me not to write a story. I felt totally crushed.

For the first – and certainly not the last – time I was experiencing the rank hypocrisy of the British Left, its essentially devious nature... and endless capacity for betrayal.

Some years later, during a protracted and Marxist-led newspaper strike, I would endure three months without pay and then final abandonment by the armchair generals of the National Union of Journalists.

From then on, I became neither left nor right-wing, but a confirmed and card-carrying no-winger. As the late Andy Warhol so astutely observed, labels are for tins, not people.

On another occasion, Geoff Ambler told me to get on my scooter and travel across town to visit relatives and inquire about the welfare of former *Teens and 20s* reporter Jim Humphreys – who had experienced some kind of family upset – and then to report back.

But for once I made a stand. I refused, saying that if he was genuinely concerned for his erstwhile colleague, he would make the effort to find out for himself.

This minor rebellion could have landed me in deep trouble and possible victimisation. But fellow reporters Dave Berry and John Burke-Davies nobly leapt to my defence and both Len and Geoff Ambler eventually climbed down.

It was one thing to be their skivvy, constantly fetching sausage rolls from the bakery, making tea and taking their betting slips down to the bookies. But I was not a total slave that had to do my masters' bidding without question and conform to their every whim.

I would later realise that this exchange had been a classic example of right-wing behaviour masked by a leftist moral conceit.

However, from now on, my card was most definitely marked. Taking into account this heated exchange I was just relieved that I had recently signed my apprenticeship indentures.

And although sport may well have been my weakest link, I was slowly but surely becoming an all-round reporter with the skills to match, especially when it came to feature-based pieces. The balance of power was slowly changing and moving in my direction.

I always knew that the public would eventually tire of endless council reports that ceaselessly chronicled the twitterings of mainly pompous elderly men and crusty, creaking old women.

It was quite obvious that pop writing would very much enjoy a future. Maybe not for me, as it turned out, but a number of journalists from my generation would go on to fame and occasionally notoriety as doyens of the new counter-culture… young men such as Charles Shaar Murray and Daventry-born Steve Turner.

I met Steve on one occasion when he dropped by the front office and asked to talk to me about some poems he'd written. Little did I know then that Steve would one day be at the top of his game as a poet and writer.

I can't stress enough how perplexing all this was to anyone aged over 30. Before the dawn of rock and roll, the populace existed in a dark night of mainly Italiano-American pap, oily ballads almost always sung with a conspicuous lack of conviction by men with even greasier hair and wearing tight-fitting, bum-freezing shiny suits.

The advent of Elvis Presley and his countless imitators changed all that. Music was no longer an accompaniment to life… it was becoming the way of life for millions of people. And I was glad to be one of them.

No wonder then that Len Archer and Geoff Ambler were left in a state of utter bewilderment and not a little resentment… and how my life must have contrasted with theirs.

For example, I would wake up in the morning and pile a stack of shiny, vinyl singles on to the turntable of my green Dansette record player in my bedroom.

No doubt Len and Geoff just tuned into the BBC's Light Programme and after hearing the shipping forecast would don hat and coat, pick up their sandwiches, bid farewell to respective wives, and head off once more to work.

Not me. The day began and ended many hours later to the sound of rock and roll. I lived off a daily diet of pop, rock, blues, soul, jazz and folk.

And this was the fundamental difference between them and us. They just about tolerated the new journalism but never attached any value to it.

When I look back over the years, I think that they both had very little regard for what would later come to be recognised as standard news reporting, the kind that we take for granted now, but back in the 1960s was truly revolutionary.

'Celebrity' didn't exist as a concept. If you were a journalist who classed everyone who didn't wear a sports jacket, cavalry twills, Oxford brogues and had something other than a short back and sides haircut as being a 'long-haired layabout' then that didn't leave much room for manoeuvre.

But how could the worth of a story be calculated purely from a person's outward appearances… surely this was not the much coveted 'news sense' that appeared to be so highly prized?

To their way of thinking, if I didn't share their view of what constituted tried and tested story subjects, then I wasn't to be admitted to their club of tired old hacks on countdown to retirement. It was hard going at times, I can tell you. And that story's never been written, incidentally.

What Len and Geoff didn't seem to understand or recognise was the fact that my page led every week with an off-diary piece that I'd picked up in a pub or dance hall.

Possibly worst of all for them, I was determinedly ploughing my own furrow and living my young life as I wanted to. And what's more, I was loving every single minute of it. No wonder then that The Who's 'Hope I die before I get old' lyric had a certain resonance.

It was around this time that I made my first visit to Swinging London. I had been to the capital city once before, during my childhood, when I had been taken on a trip to London Zoo by my father.

But this was different. I would be travelling alone. Gulp. How would I cope with the tube system?

So. Picture a lad from rural Warwickshire, suitcase heavy in my hand, packed with more clothes than I could ever hope to wear in a single weekend.

It was a spring day in 1967… the legendary merry month of May, if my memory serves me correctly. The sun hung high in the heavens on this fabulous morning, no doubt glinting in the Beatle-esque mop top of hair that clung to my head like some kind of furry helmet.

This was how Dick Whittington must have felt, I mused, as the train pulled out of Rugby Midland station and began the 80-mile journey to the centre of the Universe. London…

Not yet aged 18, my sister had arranged to meet me at Euston to ensure I negotiated the labyrinth of the Tube, an adventure all in itself. At some stage, with the hot breath of the Underground still on our necks, we emerged at Stockwell, and walked the few hundred yards to my sister's flat in South Lambeth.

Even then, every yard of the way seemed to drench the senses. So this was it… the fabled swinging London, capital of the alternative culture, and the ultimate in everything that was hip.

My sister lived with her boyfriend and that in itself was then considered utterly outrageous by most people over 30.

We arrived at her pad. On the walls of the flat were the standard posters of that period – there was Che Guevara looking into the middle distance, no doubt plotting another revolution from beyond the grave, and next to him were the high kickers of the Moulin Rouge.

Years later, by a truly strange coincidence, some friends were to live next door – and my sister's house would be owned by television star Joanna Lumley. But back then, the building was divided into flats, a communal hall with peeling paintwork hinting at a faded grandeur.

That night I sampled curry for the first time. Such food was virtually unknown in provincial Britain in those days, although Chinese restaurants had started to make an appearance on high streets.

It was also the first time that I had tasted red wine, too. Such fare is, of course, now commonplace, but in 1967 was considered rather adventurous and exotic.

The next day, we went into 'town'. Unlike Dick Whittington, I didn't expect the streets to be paved with gold, but they were certainly thronged with some very colourful-looking characters.

The first call was The King's Road, an area that appeared to be populated by hippy lords and ladies, a new aristocracy of the streets, resplendent in their coats of many colours and regulation long hair.

Then it was on to Berwick Street Market, and who should be plying his musical wares, but Don Partridge the busker. It would be only a few months after this sighting that he would shoot to the top of the pop charts with *Rosie*.

I remember his 'bottler', an elfin girl with a yellow, corn shock of hair who weaved her way through the crowds collecting coins and the occasional pound note.

I vividly recall Don in his snakeskin jacket, blue jeans, gypsy hair and a single earring. He was a natural street musician, holding his battered acoustic Gibson guitar high to maximise its projection and volume.

Talking of guitars, Portobello Road seemed to have a finger-picker on every corner, playing what I would later come to recognise as blues and ragtime styles.

And as if this bewildering assault on the senses wasn't enough, no trip to Swinging London in the 1960s would have been complete without a walk down Carnaby Street, then the most fashionable thoroughfare in the Western hemisphere.

Near the legendary Biba, we found Lord John's, where, after much deliberation, I bought a velvet military-style tunic. It was black with red collar, cuffs and epaulettes.

More than 50 years later, I still have this musty-smelling garment, a souvenir of that long-lost London weekend in the 60s.

Britain's capital was basking in a golden age. London was the glorious centrepiece of a country that had just relinquished the last vestiges of empire.

The old girl was letting her greying locks down and partying to celebrate the end of centuries-old domination and global responsibility. The more troubled 70s were still some way off, and even further away lay the drab decades of strife and international terrorism.

But all this was yet to happen. Back in that summer of 1967, for a certain wide-eyed lad from the Midlands, London was a fabulous, mythical place where the streets – if not exactly coated in the shiny stuff – were paved with my good intentions, at least.

Charlie was our darling

FOR a man who spent the vast majority of his life indoors, Charlie Field certainly had a remarkable sun tan.

And a fine head of hair, too. With not a hint of a widow's peak, the hairline started in perfect alignment on the brim of his forehead, the lustrous locks then sent cascading back, forming rivulets of 1950s pop star-style brylcreemed jet-black waves that might have even won an admiring glance from Elvis Presley himself.

And to top it all off, Charlie's crowning glory was gloriously complimented by a perfect row of gleaming, white teeth which completed what was literally a living, walking and talking painting in oils… only in his case, various hair oils and pomade.

Plus, of course, a regular top-up coating of Man Tan, in those days a popular bottled product among those who coveted an all-year coating of dusky facial veneer.

Small wonder then that Charlie liked to smile a lot. And by that, I really mean a great deal. He could turn on the charm with the same amount of effort it would take you or me to switch on a light.

When Charlie welcomed you to his regal presence, it was a burst of radiance that instantly informed the beholder that they were in the company of showbiz royalty.

Well, that's probably how Charlie saw it. But in truth, Charlie was actually a large fish in a small Rugby pond. But there again, I quite understood where he was coming from, because that was essentially what I was too, only in another line of work.

Charlie Field was the manager of the Granada Cinema in North Street. Sorry, correction – the Granada THEATRE in North Street. Because that's how he liked to regard his empire of sound and moving pictures that once stood in all its majestic grandeur on the bend in the road opposite Rugby Town Hall.

And to a large degree, Charlie was entitled to regard himself as a bit of an impresario, because in those days, cinemas were not just darkened caverns where people went to see the latest films.

When Music Hall died and was replaced by 'variety' shows, the local cinema was often the only venue left to accommodate touring pop groups, comedians, jugglers and acrobats.

In the 1960s, unless they were absolute blockbusters, most films stayed for only a week in provincial cinemas. These 'flicks' would be accompanied by a 'b' picture, usually either a Western or a horror movie filmed in monochrome.

Aiming for a young demographic, such improbable dramas would invariably have ludicrous titles, such as *Plague of the Teenage Zombies,* a ridiculous film I vividly recall seeing one winter's Sunday afternoon.

And in order to further cash in on the burgeoning youth market, cinema managers across Britain started to feature not just touring chart groups but also local rock talent, too.

Among the many local bands that regularly appeared on the Granada stage were the Surf Cyders, Sam Spade and the Gravediggers, The Liberators and the Ravens.

As for me, I was developing an insatiable appetite for anything to do with what many might now loftily refer to as the performing arts. My life had become an endless round of attending events, many of them connected with the stage.

Writing an entire broadsheet page devoted to show news meant that I had to constantly trawl the Rugby area for stories, literally mixing business with pleasure. It was a dream come true… sometimes, I felt as if I needed to pinch myself.

And Charlie was not slow in cottoning on to the activities of this young upstart crow who had been given so much power on the *Rugby Advertiser* after so little time in the job. And that's why he was invariably on the phone, hoping to attract me to one of his publicity stunts.

And as far as these were concerned, Charlie was an expert. He had the publicist's eye when it came to plugging something. Although the Granada had publicised Westerns as long ago as the early 1950s – involving a Stetson-wearing, sixgun-toting 'cowboy' who rode through Rugby on a horse – Charlie Field took the whole concept quite a few steps further.

His preferred modus operandi was to stage a publicity stunt on the steps of the Granada. This would follow a familiar theme, one that echoed the general thrust of a given film.

Whenever an event was being staged, he would ring me up and ask if the *Advertiser* could cover it. The answer was always yes, because Charlie was no fool, and had managed to become a personal friend of the Editor. So basically, saying 'no' to Charlie was out of the question.

But one Saturday morning, I was present at a stunt which went seriously wrong. Somehow or other, Charlie had managed to persuade a local farmer to 'lend' him a flock of sheep to publicise a film – its title now escapes me – that must have had an agricultural flavour.

The sheep were penned as you might expect. But half way through the proceedings, and undoubtedly panicking because of all the human attention, one of the animals reared up and broke through the fencing.

And that was it. Sheep being sheep, the others followed through and before anyone realised what was happening, the entire flock was running up North Street, forcing vehicles to a standstill and pedestrians to take evasive action.

This was obviously a good news story. What had begun as potential material for my page was now a cracking tale destined for the news pages and that's how it was presented, complete with pictures, in the next edition of the *Advertiser*.

I fully expected Charlie to ring up and complain, or even march up to Albert Street and see his friend the Editor in person. But no. Charlie was a good-hearted chap and, unlike a lot of movers and shakers in the town, understood that sometimes the publicity game didn't always go the way you wanted it to.

But despite all of Charlie's pretensions, the Rugby Granada was actually a bit of a fleapit. It was an old brick building built in 1933, and originally called the Plaza, but changed its name in 1946 in the same way as so many others, as they borrowed continental place names such as the Rialto or Alhambra to make them sound more exotic and exciting.

Long before I was taking a professional interest in the Granada, in the 1950s, I briefly joined The Rugby Grenadiers, a Charlie Field brainchild intended to get 'em young and win over the adult cinemagoer of the future.

The inside of the Granada was dark and smelled of stale cigarette smoke. But despite this unprepossessing atmosphere, once you had sat down in your seat, you were transported to a land of fantasy and fun.

The seats were covered in a sort of maroon velveteen, which for small boys wearing short trousers, soon made your legs itch. I suppose the girls must have had a similar problem with their dresses and skirts.

But the one thing that really sticks in my mind was how the noise levels could reach astronomic heights as around 300 children aged between five and 13 screamed, whistled, shouted and booed at any and every opportunity.

To try and keep some sort of order, Charlie had an ace up his sleeve, which was to give out shillings to children who were sitting still and temporarily behaving themselves.

Throughout the show, cinema staff would pass through the building and randomly hand out the coins to children who were seemingly behaving themselves.

Mind you, once you had that shilling in your sweaty little palm, you could pretty much behave as badly as you liked. And as soon as they had all been given out, it was absolute bedlam.

When a Western feature was showing, it was customary for small boys to come dressed for the part. This meant arriving at the Granada complete with check shirt, cowboy hat, and gun belt with holstered Lone Star six-shooters, the weapon of choice for most small boys in those days.

As with all Westerns of the period, there would be frequent chase sequences, always either the 'goodies' after the 'baddies' or stagecoaches being pursued by hostile Indians.

Whenever this happened, out would come several hundred pistols and the air would be filled with the crackle of gunfire and the distinctive smell of 'cap' smoke. It was brilliant fun and utter chaos.

On one occasion, a boy actually took an air pistol into the cinema and started firing at random during the film, a crime which only came to light when members of staff noticed that small holes were suddenly starting to appear in the screen.

Charlie Field was undoubtedly one of Rugby's great characters during the 1960s. He spoke in a high-pitched, rather 'posh' voice that was almost certainly not his own, was married to a truly voluptuous lady called Renate, and had made Rugby and its cinema his life.

By the 1970s, audience numbers were dwindling, and the Granada finally closed its doors on February 28, 1976. The final showing featured Paul Newman and Steve McQueen in, perhaps fittingly, the disaster picture *The Towering Inferno.*

The building was converted into a Granada Bingo Club, which in May 1991 become a Gala Bingo Club. The building was put up for sale in 2007. But three years later in November, 2010, it was announced that the Gala Bingo Club would be closing the next month.

Tragically, this fine building was demolished in November, 2011. And with it, as far as I was concerned, went a whole host of happy memories, not least of which was working with the irrepressible Charlie Field, he of the permanent sun tan and jet-black dyed hair.

An iron fist and constitution to match

THE London House in Chapel Street was one of several favoured watering holes for *Advertiser* reporters.

There was just one female journalist in the editorial office and that was Jenny Ferguson. Miss Ferguson hailed from Pontefract in Yorkshire and was a university graduate.

This, combined with the adoption of a slightly vague, middle class air, firmly set her aside from those of us in steerage class. She probably only visited the London House on a couple of occasions as it would have appeared to her as being a bit of a dive.

Nevertheless, the pub was a respectable hostelry that catered for a broad range of ordinary working people. It was run by Tom Rotherham and his wife Mary. She did the cooking, serving up simple fare such as chicken or steak and kidney pie, chips and mushy peas.

The *Advertiser* was 'put to bed' late on Thursday afternoons and it was the custom to visit the London House towards the end of the week when the bulk of the work had been done.

The pub was frequented by a number of local characters, by far the most interesting and unusual being Carl Dane. He had worked as the original 'gong man' for the Rank Organisation's films.

Many of the early films produced by Rank feature Carl Dane. He was a former circus strongman and certainly lived up to that role when I first met him.

He had a number of party tricks, the most impressive being his ability to crush a cooking apple to a pulp with one hand. Another stunt involved hammering a six-inch nail into a block of wood with his clenched fist, using only a handkerchief to soften the blows and thereby avoid physical damage.

I clearly remember being introduced, shaking hands with Carl, and feeling the sheer power of his grip. It reminded me of the *Tom and Jerry* cartoons where the characters' bones and teeth would often comically crumble into piles of tiny fragments.

Carl Dane was a heavy drinker, consuming up to 25 pints of beer a day, and could drain a glass in a single sucking motion.

I had never seen anything like it. He would down a pint in two or three seconds and then wander up to the bar for a refill. He spent most of his waking hours at the London House, regaling customers with his stories, and undoubtedly helped to maintain a steady income for Tom and Mary.

Another local character was Ron Ferriday, who looked like an aging Second World War spiv and quite likely had been one. He wore a crumpled, brown pinstripe suit, and sported a thin black moustache that stretched like a rather thin, malnourished slug reclining across his top lip.

Ron was very much the 'wide boy' and his penchant for drink must have caused his family quite a lot of grief. On one occasion, he was arrested by the police for being drunk in charge of his car. He had driven across the front garden lawns of not just his own house, but also that of his neighbours'.

This was before Barbara Castle's drink-driving laws were passed in 1967. Before then, the police would make the suspect walk along a straight white line drawn in chalk in the station back yard. If you veered away from the line that would then prove you were drunk.

These visits to the London House firmly acquainted me with the joys or otherwise of alcoholic beverages. Despite the fact that I was not yet aged 18, I had been actively encouraged by Len and the other reporters to drink beer… and lots of it, on occasion. As a result of this, I would soon become unstuck.

Before long I had developed a taste for beer and cider. One night, after a heavy session in the bar at the Benn Hall, I climbed on my scooter and tried to drive to my family home in Churchover.

I didn't get very far. At around three in the morning, I was woken by two policemen who had found me fast asleep on the central reservation of the Leicester Road underneath a Rugby landmark, a railway viaduct known as the Eleven Arches.

It was pouring with rain, I was soaked to the skin… and all I could hear was this policeman's voice asking who I was. They had responded to a call from a member of the public who had reported a scooter parked in the middle of the carriageway.

Jolting awake, I told the officers that I was not drunk but 'prone to blackouts'. This didn't cut any ice with the policemen, one of them saying, over and again: *"You're pissed, John!"*

They then took me in their land rover to Rugby Police Station, where I was interviewed by a kindly sergeant. Once again, I stuck to my 'blackouts' line and he seemed to swallow this ridiculous lie, although I'm pretty sure he didn't believe a word.

Nevertheless, luck – and my guardian angel, no doubt – came to the rescue and I was taken home rather than being charged with anything. I would have got home around four in the morning and my mother had to get out of bed to let me in the house.

Lying through her teeth, she corroborated my ludicrous fiction, and the sergeant soon went on his way, his parting words being: "You need to look after your lad if he's prone to blackouts, madam."

To this day, I think the main reason why I was let off the hook was because the sergeant could see that I came from a respectable family and had probably learnt my lesson.

The problem was that I hadn't, of course. And there would be several more occasions when drink almost caused my downfall.

Barely four hours after being brought home in a police car, I found myself back at my desk on the *Advertiser,* bleary-eyed and badly hung over. Then a few minutes later, Len burst through the door, grinning from ear to ear.

He had just called at the police station, a routine daily practice, to check whether anything of importance had happened overnight. And it had… a drama concerning me.

Len could hardly contain himself. He said that the duty sergeant had told him about my escapades during the night, and spluttering through his laughter, said: "And when the coppers woke you up as you lay on the grass on the central reservation, you said 'morning mum, what's for breakfast?'"

I had imagined that I would be for the high jump if my misdemeanours had been uncovered, but on the contrary, for Len was high amused.

Len Archer was indeed a dichotomy. On the one hand he could be the stern, humourless and sometimes bullying taskmaster, on the other a former wayward lad himself and laughing at potentially humorous incidents… especially if they involved alcohol.

Despite being underage, and actively encouraged to drink by the other reporters, I do recall being hypocritically admonished by Geoff Ambler on one occasion when we returned from yet another session at the London House.

Ignoring the fact that Len was not only as guilty as anyone – he was my mentor as far as such matters were concerned – Geoff Ambler rounded on me as I once again stumbled through the reporters' room door, saying: "Why do you want Tom Rotherham to lose his licence, lad?"

This was totally unfair. Len, a man of twice my age, and a senior member of staff, had wanted me to be a member of his drinking club. Yes, I discovered that I had a taste for it, but at the same time felt pressure to fit in with the rest of the crew.

It was a case of being damned if you do and damned if you don't. These days, an adult encouraging a minor to drink beer would probably be contravening some law or other.

I can clearly remember Len's habit of dropping in to a pub 'for a swift half' on his way back from police calls.

One day, I accompanied him to the police station, and on the return journey, he knocked on the door of the Seven Stars in nearby James Street.

It was just 10 o'clock in the morning, and this was early, even by today's standards of 24-hour opening. Anyway, a cautious sounding voice came from behind the door, inquiring who it was and what they wanted.

"It's me, Len," said the decidedly thirsty chief reporter, in a half-whisper. The door was duly opened.

The landlord moved behind the bar, knowing full well what his customer wanted. "I'll have a half of bitter. Oh yes, and pull one for the boy, too." I was still aged only 16.

The Squirrel… Rugby's oldest pub.

Excessive and occasional illegal drinking could also make the news columns. In those days, Britain was subject to quite strict licensing laws, legislation that had been passed as far back as the First World War when the authorities had become concerned about the drinking habits of women munitions workers.

Drunkenness posed a threat to safety in factories where the risk of explosions was always present, and so draconian laws were passed so that workers' consumption was limited by time. Even by the 1960s, these laws had not been repealed. That would come much later.

The hours that licensed premises could be open were strictly controlled across the land, although there were anomalies. For example, it was possible to have a last drink in a Warwickshire hostelry, get into your car, and race over the border to Northamptonshire, where the pubs were open half an hour later.

And then there were the famous 'lock-ins' whereby the landlord might close his pub to the public, bolt the door, and allow 'friends' to keep buying and consuming alcohol.

If challenged by the police, the landlord could say that he was entertaining 'guests' in his 'home' and was therefore not subject to any licensing laws.

However, that didn't always work. Such as the time that almost the entire adult population of Churchover was hauled before the Rugby magistrates accused of consuming alcoholic liquor after hours in a licensed premises, namely the Greyhound Inn.

Mercifully, Len Archer excused me court duty that day. It would have been rather embarrassing, to say the least.

Friday afternoons were set aside for shorthand lessons. This was not necessarily good planning, bearing in mind the nature and duration of that day's lunch break. In fact, the timing couldn't have been worse.

Not only was my concentration impaired as a result of being awash with beer, but I had to frequently break off from the class in order to visit the gents' lavatory.

Our teacher was the wife of John Hardeman, the *Coventry Evening Telegraph's* district reporter in Rugby. She was a very kind, understanding and gracious woman, a far cry from her husband who frequently crossed swords with *Advertiser* reporters.

The clashes usually occurred over the issue of shared reporting arrangements. This was a system whereby jobs were often covered for both papers because of a reporter's day off or illness.

It was a sort of gentleman's agreement. But the problem was that John often seemed to forget about his side of the bargain, and any idea of reciprocation might suddenly fly out of the *Telegraph* window when the time came to ask a favour of him.

Things came to a head one day when I was running copy for a sports reporter covering a Rugby Lions home match. 'Running copy' entailed a second journalist phoning across a pre-ordered story to the away team's home paper.

The usual arrangement was so many words after 25 minutes, another bulletin at half-time, and the final result being sent immediately after the end of the match. As there was only one phone box at Rugby's Webb Ellis ground, it was a case of first come, first served.

Just after half-time, I had reached the box and was starting to file copy when I was startled by a violent knocking on the glass. It was John Hardeman.

"How long will you be?" he barked. "I'll be as quick as possible," I replied.

A minute or two elapsed and the hammering started again. This time I was less patient and told him that the more he hit the door, the longer it would take for me to finish phoning.

By now, his face had reddened, and I could sense that these exchanges were going to end badly.

The hammering started again. And this time, I completely lost it. I asked the copytaker in Pontypridd to wait a moment, grabbed John Hardeman by the lapels, and threatened all manner of physical retribution if he didn't desist from his unreasonable interruptions.

That seemed to do the trick. And that, as far as I was concerned, was the end of it… until I was summoned into John Lawson's office on the Monday morning.

I was then informed in no uncertain manner that I was not to swear at, let alone threaten, Mr Hardeman with physical violence.

Now, I didn't so much mind the telling-off, but the fact that Hardeman had 'snitched' – I was little more than a grammar school boy, remember – seemed to go against all notions of gentlemanly honour.

This wouldn't have happened at my old school, I thought. John Hardeman surely couldn't have been a grammar school boy, I mused with a lofty sense of grandeur. Better a thrashing than dishonour.

A few weeks later, my colleague Dave Berry also had a run-in with the man from the *Telegraph*. He'd asked John Hardeman if he could share his dining table at the nearby Venture Café. All the other chairs were taken.

The Venture Café was used quite a lot by both the staff at the *Advertiser* and *Telegraph* offices.

But John Hardeman refused the request. This resulted in Dave swearing at him and storming out. And once again, a complaint was made to Mr Lawson, and Dave was hauled over the still warm coals that I had only recently trodden.

John Hardeman was a snappy dresser, invariably wearing a bow tie. He was a Rugby railwayman's son and had left school at 14. Like me, he had been apprenticed to the *Rugby Advertiser* at what would now be regarded as a very young age.

He would ultimately go on to forge a successful career for himself, rising to the rank of group editor for Worcestershire's Berrows Newspapers.

Years later, I would join this company as a sub-editor on the *Evesham Journal*. On the Wednesday of my first week at the paper, I travelled to Worcester to put the paper 'to bed'.

I walked into the composing room… and there was John Hardeman. He purposely strode over to me and introduced himself, knowing full well that we'd known each other all those years before.

But he obviously wanted to erase the past, to wipe the slate clean… to start our relationship anew. But that was John Hardeman. He died in April, 2018, at the age of 84, dapper to the last.

One night in the summer of 1967, I met up with former schoolmate Chris James, who had been apprenticed as a printer on the *Advertiser* at the same time that I'd been taken on.

Chris was with a couple of friends. After a night of drinking at the Raglan Arms, we started off through town, with nothing particular being planned.

But it wasn't long before disaster struck, when one of our party smashed the plate glass window of a wine shop in Church Street and grabbed several bottles of booze.

Completely bewildered and not knowing what to do, I decided that the best course of action was to rapidly vacate the scene. But it wasn't long before the police arrived and we were all arrested.

Once we had arrived at the police station, we were split up and separately interrogated by detective constables. I really thought that my luck had run out this time, but no – my good fortune held out when my companions swore that I had done nothing wrong and was just an unwilling witness to what had happened.

The others admitted what they had done. So I was released and then walked the four miles back to my home in Churchover.

I finally reached my destination at around five in the morning, snatching a couple of hours' sleep before going in to work. Convinced that my job might well be on the line, I came clean and told Geoff Ambler what had happened the night before.

For once, he came up with goods, saying that instead of being an accomplice to a crime, "I could say that I was reporting on the scene of a crime as it took place, a journalist on the spot just doing his job."

Once again, I had fallen head-first into a steaming muck heap and miraculously emerged smelling of violets. By now, I really felt that someone was watching over me.

But there was, of course, a common denominator here… and that was my over-enthusiastic consumption of alcohol. And while it was as much to do with me as the encouragement of Len and the others, this crash course on drinking in a working situation certainly didn't help.

Let the old good times roll

TOM Ward was an old friend of my father's who had led a dance band in Rugby since the early 1930s.

My dad had played violin with the band for a time. By the mid-1960s, Tom was virtually blind and, together with his wife Miriam, was running the Alexandra Arms pub in James Street.

By then, his all-consuming interest had become the Rugby Theatre that had been founded in the late 1940s by a number of local people, one of whom was my father.

Tom was an expert on 1930s and 40s dance band music. One afternoon I called round at the Alexandra Arms to interview him for an article on my show page which by then was carrying quite a lot of news about theatres in the Rugby area.

Tom was at that time producing a week-long run of the classic musical *Oklahoma!* And although the interview mainly concerned itself with the show, we soon drifted into a conversation about the music of Tom's younger days.

I was then a fanatical devotee of black American blues, country, folk, rock, and also keenly followed the musical progress of the many pop groups that were then dominating not just the newspaper headlines but also forming the backdrop to most people's lives.

However, Tom introduced me to something quite different. And when I heard the music of Al Bowlly, Lew Stone and Roy Fox, I became hooked on

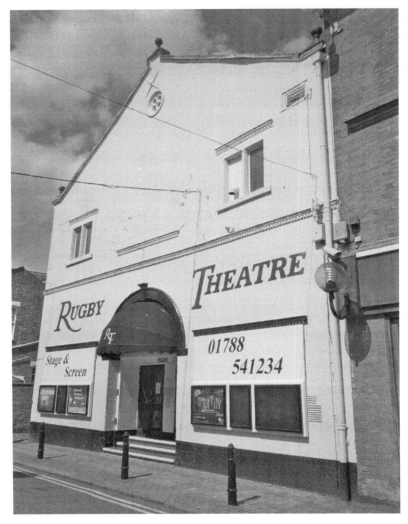

Rugby Theatre.

this, too... entranced by the sounds that had bewitched an entire generation of young people before their hopes and dreams were to be dashed away by the outbreak of war in 1939.

There was such a wistful, romantic and shamelessly sentimental feel to these old tunes, with their chocolate smooth horn sections, sweeping strings and impossibly relaxed and languid vocals of the crooners who fronted these long-lost bands.

Not long after our meeting, I came across an entire collection of 78rpm records from that era, and eagerly added them to my already burgeoning collection of vinyl singles and long players.

In those days, most record players – this was before the age of stereo – had a 78rpm option which you accessed by simply turning over to the 'green' needle on your machine. Many an hour was spent playing these old, scratchy records as I was transported back to the 1930s.

I had always been obsessed with Americana since viewing the black and white cowboy dramas on the 1950s television of my childhood. Reared on the Gene Autry and Roy Rogers songs of ranch and range, my allegiances had now turned to the black blues singers, many of whom, like the gunfighters of the Old West, had fantastically elaborate names… men such as Howling Wolf, Muddy Waters and Lightnin' Slim.

And around this time I took my first tentative steps towards learning to play this exotic music, spending hours trying to figure out the chords and how the predominantly pentatonic minor scale runs worked.

I had already sought to imitate the wailing train sound on an Echo Super Vamper harmonica, a now battered and broken instrument I'd bought as a schoolboy back in 1964 for ten shillings after seeing The Rolling Stones perform at Rugby's Granada picture house.

Brian Jones' harmonica style had captured my imagination, the sound stirring my soul to such an extent that I simply had to possess one of these magical devices, the music of which seemed to well up from the very depths of existence.

But a lot of water would flow beneath the Avon Mill bridge before I mastered the black arts of the Devil's music. And in the meantime, I honed my writing skills, which seemed to be improving as each day passed.

My show page was now becoming extremely popular throughout Rugby and district. The paper came back from the printing press to Albert Street late on a Thursday evening and I was flattered, not to say a little astonished, to hear from local disc jockey Alan Longstaff that such was the appetite for *The John Phillpott Feature* that youngsters would regularly try to get hold of that week's paper the night before it officially became available.

Alan Longstaff had a residency at the Woolpack Inn, a pub in Union Street. Sad to say, there is no sign of it these days, having been bulldozed several years ago to make way for a car park.

Yet back in the 1960s, the Woolpack had been one of the top musical hot spots in the town. The highlight of the week was Beat Club 64, held every Thursday night in the pub's top room.

The resident group was The Cataracts, but occasionally bigger names graced the rickety stage, including Cliff Bennett and the Rebel Rousers, Chris Farlowe and the Thunderbirds, and also blues and boogie piano players such as Champion Jack Dupree and Eddie Boyd.

Champion Jack's parents had been murdered by the Ku Klux Klan and he had subsequently fled Louisiana, America, for the relative safety of Halifax, Yorkshire, England.

The United States' loss was our gain. He was a highly entertaining individual who, when not playing in his distinctive, rolling New Orleans style, regaled the audience with his risqué humour while at the same time leering at any pretty girl who caught his eye.

The Cataracts were led by Roger Meakin, who eagerly rocked the joint pounding away on a Vox organ and bawling out one 1950s rock classic after another.

And did that place rock. Health and safety rules would have closed the place in an instant nowadays because the floor bounced and heaved like a ship's deck as sweating dancers stomped their way through such vintage items as Little Richard's *Ready Teddy, Rip It Up, Blue Suede Shoes* and other classics that even in 1965 really belonged to a bygone age.

The Woolpack Inn was an authentic, no-holds-barred rock and roll joint where young people regularly gathered to drink, dance and meet people of the opposite sex.

Oh yes, and also to smoke cigarettes without running the risk of parental disapproval. This was an era yet to be policed by the health fascists, a more relaxed and less uptight world in which the jackboot of political correctness had yet to grind its heel into people's faces.

One week, I deputised for Alan Longstaff and took over the disc jockey's chair for the night. I did quite well at spinning the discs and churning out the 'chat', which prompted legendary Rugby DJ Tony 'Big' Fry to ask me to join him and share the turntables at the Raglan Arms for the Wednesday night disco session.

My life was becoming jam-packed with commitments and every evening was either taken up doing night jobs for the *Advertiser* or spinning records for public consumption. In addition, I'd landed a paid gig at the London House, rather extravagantly and memorably billed as 'Tonight! John and his Guitar'.

You might well ask how I managed to do all this and also study the required art of shorthand wherever possible. The answer to that question is simple. This was the 1960s and many of us were driving in the proverbial fast lane, with the stick firmly stuck in top gear.

Amazingly, I very rarely felt tired, such was my zest for life. And by the way, that appalling cliché and much-used saying 'if you remember the 60s then you weren't there' is total hogwash.

Yes, there may have been instances which elude recall, but in the main, I remember that period with crystal-clear clarity. The facts of the matter are that a year in the 1960s was worth three of any other decade, before or since.

In this period of the 20th century there were no more wars to fight and – crucially – no compulsory National Service to get in the way and hinder our hedonism. And my generation certainly made the most of it… we were truly blessed without a doubt.

But the best thing of all was that I was doing the only job that my unremarkable and fractured schooling had equipped me for… the privilege of being a journalist on my home town's newspaper.

Don't get the wrong end of the stick

WE live in a world dominated by computers. But it wasn't always the case, and the newspaper industry is a textbook example of what working life was like before the arrival of the new technology.

The *Rugby Advertiser's* official address may have been Albert Street, but the operation also sprawled across Gas Street into the printing works, a cavernous building that later became a pub chain's outlet known as The Rupert Brooke.

The *Advertiser,* like all papers in those days, was printed by means of what was termed the hot metal process. Copy was set on linotype or monotype machines that rattled and clattered away as their operators followed the advertising reps' requirements or sub-editors written instructions on the reporters' stories.

The type itself was a blend of lead and a metal called antimony, the latter being included to introduce a hardening element.

Headlines were usually set on a machine known universally as a 'Ludlow' and pictures were reproduced employing a photo-sensitive process that transferred the image to a metal plate that was then attached to a wooden 'block'.

The compositor then took all these components and painstakingly followed the page plan instructions, fitting everything together on a metal frame, which in turn was supported by an extremely sturdy and heavy table known as 'the stone'.

This was so-named because originally, that's exactly what it had been… a structure carved out of solid rock, the only material that could withstand the enormous weight of the metal type.

The compositor worked at what appeared to be lightning speed, moving the lines of body type into their allotted positions. Sometimes, and especially as publication day approached, the sub-editor was required to edit the material in the frame, on-the-hoof as it were.

Usually, if the type over-ran the space, or if it dropped short, some quick thinking on the part of the journalist was necessary. If it was the latter, then a 'filler' story from a 'gash' frame was dropped in the space. 'Gash' was the term for unplaced stories kept in reserve for just such an eventuality.

Both the compositor and journalist had to be able to read reversed type, although comps would often help out slow or non-readers and 'pull' a 'galley' proof by inking the relevant area with a stick, and getting an impression by placing a sheet of paper on the type and then moving a roller across it.

Incidentally, this process is the origin of the saying that alludes to someone 'getting the wrong end of the stick', in other words, they've picked up the inked end by mistake.

There was one lesson that had to be learnt quickly as far as printers were concerned and that was the paramount importance of keeping on the right side of them.

Some journalists never cottoned on to this throughout an entire working life and regularly paid the price of dealing with a surly, resentful 'inky' who – possibly already burdened with a large chip on his shoulder – certainly didn't appreciate being talked down to by a white collar office worker who was far too big for his boots.

Treat them as equals, engage in friendly conversation, ask about their lives… and you were slowly accepted. This is not as patronising as it sounds. Printers had good reason to dislike haughty hacks who thought they were a cut above.

I learnt to rub along with printers early on in my career and I'd like to think that the men 'over the road' also took a liking to me, too.

Malcolm Crick, Ron Barton, brothers Ray and Les Leeson… I often sought their company during the days when I ate sandwiches in the office rather than spending lunchtime in the pub.

Ray Leeson's face was pitted all over as a result of an accident at work. He'd been setting copy on his linotype when rainwater dripped through a hole in the factory roof and came into contact with the molten metal in the furnace of his machine.

This produced a small but violent explosion, the red-hot metal flying in all directions, much of it spraying into his face.

The furnace was fed by a yard-long silvery ingot of lead and antimony attached to a stout chain which was gradually lowered as the metals melted and were being transformed into lines of type.

This was why the linotype was so-named. Before this invention in the 1890s, each letter or 'character' had to be set by hand, the compositor using tweezers.

One can only imagine how laborious this must have been and the great attention to detail that was required on the part of the worker on a 19th century newspaper as he arranged seven point body type slowly spreading across an ocean of broadsheet pages.

The language of printers and journalists, hitherto unknown outside the industry, are now in common parlance, thanks to the computer revolution.

Some terms, however, have not crossed over into the public mainstream... words such as flong, pica, mutton, ems and ens, the latter being the form of measurement used by all papers. Column widths obviously varied from paper to paper, but were generally somewhere between nine and 12 ems. Logically, an 'en' was half an 'em'.

'Bastard measurement' was a term used to denote any width that didn't conform to the standard. And as for the sub-editor on a hot metal newspaper, if this wasn't enough to cope with, he or she also had to know how to 'cast off' copy, in other words to calculate what would be its length on the actual page.

Casting off used a basic mathematical method whereby the reporters' typewriters would be set to, for example, 57 spaces. Three lines of copy would then theoretically make roughly half an inch or about two centimetres of 8.5 body text roman type on a 9 point 'leading', as long as the reporter's machine was set to the correct width.

But quite a few often forgot, or couldn't be bothered to adhere to this simple rule. Persistent offenders were usually bawled out in public – and quite rightly, too – by a hardnosed, rhino-skinned sub-editor, something that would no longer be possible in these gentler, more gossamer sensitive days.

Offices in those days were much tougher environments than today's conflict-free zones. And although bullying can never ever be justified, human nature should not always be suppressed, as further problems inevitably surface at some stage in the future if sensible rules are routinely allowed to be broken.

After a swift spurt of public humiliation, it was amazing how reporters quickly started setting their typewriters correctly. It also probably helped to reduce the sub-editor's blood pressure levels as well.

And besides, the sub-editor's calculations often had to be made at lightning speed under pressure. Editors and chief sub-editors usually took this into account and were reasonably forgiving when calculations went awry. But the sub-editor was ultimately expected to be a craftsman and could – and often did – get a roasting over a miscalculation that had originally been set in motion by a careless, selfish reporter.

Years later, when I became a sub-editor myself, I quickly appreciated how important were these simple disciplines that manifestly made sense for everyone.

There was a distinctive smell to a print shop, a mixture of newsprint, ink, machine oil and cigarettes. Everybody seemed to smoke in those days, and although I held out for quite some time, I eventually succumbed to pressure from my colleagues.

And one in particular was John Burke-Davies, a hard-drinking, fiery Welshman from Abergavenny who didn't mind speaking his mind when the need arose.

He was fantastically devoted to the job, this enthusiasm only rivalled by an insatiable appetite for beer. I later discovered that he had added the 'Burke' bit to his surname because of his liking for the early 1960s TV series *Burke's Law*.

He liked to regard himself as a bit of a tough guy, and I suppose to some extent, he was.

When it came to the jobs we had to cover, I felt that council meetings were the most boring. Court hearings, on the other hand, could be interesting but also occasionally worrying.

This was because I often recognised the person standing in the dock… and they, in turn, knew me. At this stage of my life on the *Advertiser* I'd got to know quite a few of the local criminals, thanks to my regular frequenting of Rugby's numerous public houses.

The problem was that I never knew whether the defendant would be relaxed about his name and the nature of his offences appearing in print. But strange to relate, a number of the dodgiest characters hauled before the magistrates actually liked the idea of seeing their name in lights, presumably because it enhanced their street credibility and local fame.

I won't mention their names, but there were two notorious brothers from a village near Rugby who were always getting into trouble with the police.

They knew full well who I was and one Monday morning – to my utter horror – I saw their names on the court list of defendants appearing that day.

Anyway, I climbed the steps of the police station building at the bottom of Railway Terrace that morning with much trepidation. And when I reached the courtrooms, my heart sank as I saw them outside smoking cigarettes while waiting for their cases to be heard.

I caught their gaze and apprehensively approached the pair, both of whom were infamous for being Rugby 'hard men'. But to my amazement and considerable relief, both smiled in recognition, one of them saying: "Hello John. Are you covering court two? That's where we're appearing. Make sure you do a good story, eh John?"

To say I breathed a sigh of utter relief would be an understatement…

It's a long time ago now, but I seem to recall that the brothers had been charged with the supply of amphetamines, the main recreational drugs of the middle 1960s.

'Purple hearts' and 'black bombers' were first used by aircrew during the Second World War and were now being used on a wide scale by young partygoers in order to stay awake at all-night dance sessions.

The top venues for the all-nighters were Birmingham's Crazy E, Leicester's Nite Owl and the Gaffe in Banbury.

Rugby, with its central location, was ideally placed to reach these nearby venues and the new, highly mobile generation of post-war youngsters made the most of it. Coventry boasted the Matrix and Locarno ballrooms, both these dance halls featuring some of the biggest names of the times.

A friend and I saw The Who at the Matrix. As we drew up on our scooters at the traffic lights opposite the Dilke Arms on the outskirts of Coventry, Who guitarist Pete Townsend came alongside in his green Triumph Spitfire sports car.

He returned our jaw-dropping gaze with a half smile and an ultra cool nod of his head in our direction… and then the lights changed, and he had roared off in a cloud of blue smoke.

I vividly remember trying to inhale the Spitfire's exhaust fumes, such was my admiration for one of the greatest rock performers of all time.

On Saturday nights, once the Benn Hall had shut, we would often travel on our scooters over into Northamptonshire to Watford Gap service station on the recently constructed M1.

The advent of Britain's first motorway meant that the groups of the day could travel up and down the country easily. With Watford Gap situated dead centre in the middle of England, the groups invariably stopped for a late night meal on their way back to London or the north.

This would mainly take the form of a plate of greasy food washed down with endless cups of coffee and the inevitable cigarettes.

Among the members of the rock aristocracy I spotted during their offstage moments were Bill Wyman and Keith Richards of The Rolling Stones, Chris Farlowe and Dave Davies of The Kinks.

Meanwhile, Len Archer was becoming increasingly curious about the life I was leading. And in what I regarded as a deliberate attempt to compromise me, suggested that the *Advertiser* should send some undercover reporters to expose what he believed to be a thriving drugs racket at Watford Gap. And I would be included in the team, too. Then I noticed what could only be described as a malicious gleam in his eye.

I told him that he could do as he deemed fit, but would have to leave me out of any such expedition. Many of the people I was writing about not only dominated the local rock scene, but were also to be found after hours at Watford Gap.

Maybe they were taking drugs, maybe not. And so what if they did? Len Archer liked beer, didn't he? And that contains alcohol... and isn't alcohol a drug?

There was no way I was going to risk my page and – even worse – face the threat of being run out of town or lynched. Len predictably dug in his heels, perhaps thinking that he'd got me at last.

But it never came to anything. This undercover jaunt never happened and remained in Len's imagination. Meanwhile, I was left in peace to write unhindered about the renegades, reprobates and rockers of Rugby. My page was now selling papers, the adults had to wise up to this... and I wasn't afraid to fight my corner when necessary.

Square pegs in round holes

WITHIN weeks of leaving Lawrence Sheriff school I had entered what seemed to me at the time as being a surreal world populated not only by larger-than-life characters, but also individuals who plainly could never have existed in any other sphere other than that of newspapers.

For example, it would have been impossible to imagine Len Archer working in, say, a bank or building society. Can you imagine a bank manager popping out at 10 o'clock in the morning for a pint of bitter?

But in many ways, Len was the more restrained of the species. Take Percy Hepworth, for instance.

Percy was a district reporter for the *Leicester Mercury*, an evening paper that in those days circulated widely in the Rugby area. The news editors of that era had a fearsome reputation for breathing down district reporters' necks, but Percy somehow seemed immune.

He was often to be found over the Leicestershire border, covering Lutterworth magistrates' court, a task he seemed to loathe and love in equal proportions.

He would sit on the press bench, often doing a running commentary on the progress of a case, invariably making rude and derogatory comments about the defendant or the people who made up the magistrates panel.

He was particularly insulting about the clerk, a woman with red hair who studiously and stoically ignored the garrulous pressman who sat only a few feet away.

But on more than one occasion Percy was ejected by the ushers from the court room, only to return when he – not the magistrates – thought he'd been punished enough.

Percy usually turned up to court in a battered old van which also contained his pet sheepdog. The animal always sat patiently while his master was either taking notes or being thrown out of the building by court staff, who seemed to regard the problematic Percy as just another impediment to the smooth running of their day.

Nevertheless, Percy was otherwise a genial sort of chap once you got to know him. If he tired of writing down the details of a careless driving case, or jotting down the defence statements of a man who had been caught with cannabis in his car on the nearby M1, he'd put his pen down and say: "I'm bored with this bloody nonsense, lad. And I want to go to Market Harborough races to catch the 2.45. So would you cover the rest and send it to the *Mercury*? Just bill them for lineage in the usual way."

And without further ado, he'd noisily leave the room, receiving some extremely disapproving glances in the process.

Lineage was very much a major part of a provincial journalist's income in those days. Most regional reporters sent stories to other papers, from weeklies through to evenings and regularly to the nationals.

If the publication in question couldn't cover a story with one of its own staff reporters, the paper's news editor would get on the phone and ask the local man or woman to do it.

And what's more, there was good money to be earned, too. These days, stories are stolen wholesale from the internet by rival media. BBC journalists are by far the worst culprits, not only refusing to pay for tip-offs, but also lifting news items without even having the decency to check with the author.

Despite its moral posturing and often sanctimonious bearing, the BBC has no qualms whatsoever when it comes to 'lifting' stories. They do it every day of the week, a cynical process the result of which is to reduce still further the incomes of fellow journalists.

This is an utter disgrace and it's about time the public was told about what is done in the name of their ever-increasing licence money.

Many of today's media people often defend technology to the hilt. But the fact remains that pilfering another journalist's story was once regarded as a despicable crime, something no self-respecting scribbler would ever do.

Nowadays, story theft takes place every day of the week on an industrial scale, thereby adding to the general impoverishment of newspaper journalists. Not a lot of people knew that… perhaps they do now.

Walter Green was another larger-than-life character. He had originally been a cobbler from the once-great shoe town of Northampton, but after his demob from the Army after the Second World War in 1945, Walter decided on a change. So he bought an old linotype from a scrapyard.

He then taught himself to operate the machine and set to work founding a newspaper that would not only achieve great local fame but also no small degree of national notoriety as well.

The *Daventry Weekly Express* – still known as 'The Gusher' – was a success right from the start, mainly due to Walter's highly unorthodox approach to journalism.

Mixing fact with comment, the front page lead story soon became required reading for the good folk of Daventry, as all manner of dark deeds, corrupt practices and various Establishment shenanigans were unearthed by the utterly fearless Walter.

A self-taught investigative journalist, he had a reel-to-reel tape recorder wired up to his phone. Once he had enough evidence to expose something or someone, he'd set to work on his battered old Remington and metaphorically hammered nails into the coffin of the accused.

He steadfastly refused to be intimidated by anyone. Never before or since have I witnessed such editorial fearlessness, integrity and unshakeable self-belief. It was a sight to behold.

Like all good and highly principled journalists, he refused to join any organisation, association, club, society or focus group. He knew – as all professional hacks do – that the risk of entering any pact with anything or anybody will at some stage inevitably result in a clash of interest.

Walter Green bowed to no one. And that brings me to his famous meeting with the late John Algar, the Editor-in-Chief of Heart of England Newspapers, a company that is now no more, being absorbed a few years ago by one of the major conglomerates that now control the majority of local papers.

John Algar was everything that Walter wasn't, up to his neck in the Leamington Spa establishment, a member of Rotary Club, pillar of the Church and a Freemason to boot.

Heart of England bought up the *Daventry Weekly Express* sometime in the late 1960s, along with the *Rugby Advertiser*, and Walter was soon to be imperiously summoned by John Algar to the company's head office.

He duly arrived on the appointed day, knocked on the great man's door, and was met with a regal "Come!"

Walter entered the room. His eyes met with a rather small, dapper individual with a fine head of greying hair and a neatly trimmed military style pencil-thin moustache.

The man from Daventry stood on the carpet and waited. And waited… and then waited some more.

But the man he'd come to see didn't once look up, continuing to read a document of some kind. The message was very clear. *I am an extremely important person…*

It wasn't long before Walter had had enough. He took off his shoes and – bringing them down on the desk with a loud crash – said with a mischievous gleam in his eye, while employing his best Northamptonshire mangled vowels: *"Ah med them boogas misself!"*

John Algar nearly jumped out of his skin. He would not forget that meeting in a hurry.

In the summer of 1967, and also subsequently the following year, I was seconded to work for the *Express.* A few years ago I visited Daventry, but the town I knew back then seemed to have changed out of all recognition, and I failed to locate the old office where I had worked all those years ago.

But the trip did bring back a few happy memories of working with Walter. I recalled how right from the start he allowed me to write an entire page devoted to Daventry show news, a task I relished because it once again provided me with the perfect excuse to meet the local rock 'n' rollers and the amateur theatre people.

Anything was better than a constant diet of courts and councils, although I still had to report on the doings of the numerous ne'er do wells inhabiting that part of Northamptonshire.

As with Len Archer, I think I must have been a bit of a mystery to Walter, with my longish hair, ginger sideburns reaching down to my chin, and fashionable mid-1960s clothes.

But for the most part, I rubbed along with him as we sat – even by local newspaper standards – back-to-back in the tiniest office I have ever encountered.

Like me he was a smoker, his preferred brand being Kensitas. He had a fairly good head of hair for a man of his age, a tanned face despite being indoors for much of the time… and a jagged white scar on his top lip.

This had been the result of biting himself during an epileptic fit, a condition from which he had suffered for most of his adult life.

Because there were only two of us in this cramped little room, he gave me instructions on what to do should he have a fit in my presence. Luckily, this never happened.

Walter was generally very pleased with my contributions to the *Daventry Weekly Express* during those two summers, although I vaguely recall having a row with him about something or other on one occasion.

Walter and his wife – I never learnt her first name, it was always 'Mrs Green' to both of us – lived in the nearby village of Long Buckby.

But Walter was by no mean its most famous resident. That honour belonged to one Marcia Williams, the personal secretary to the then British Prime Minister Harold Wilson.

Rumours have persisted down the years about the precise nature of their relationship. But if Walter knew more than the rest of us, he most certainly wasn't telling. For that was one step that even Walter Green – erstwhile scourge of the Daventry Establishment – was not prepared to take. A countryman to his core, he obviously adhered to that good old rural saying which went… "Never sh*t up your own nest." No indeed.

Some dead men actually do tell tales

I DESCRIBED in my book *Beef Cubes and Burdock: Memories of a 1950s Country Childhood* how newspapers years ago would routinely cover road accidents, often following the ambulance in the office van.

The moment Len heard that telltale siren, he was on the phone to a police or ambulance contact to find out what was going on.

Then the phone would be slammed down and Len would say: "It's a fatal on the A5. Mike Burnett, grab your camera and take the boy. It's a bad one near Bransford Bridge.

"Boy. As soon as you have some details, get on the blower. If there's no phone box nearby, knock on someone's door and ask to use their phone."

So off we went, racing along the Leicester Road and on to the A5, the Romans' Watling Street. At the crossroads stood the Gibbet Garage, so-named because of the corpses of criminals that once hanged in cages, rotted, and provided food for the local crows.

Executed miscreants were exhibited at a crossroads because it was believed that the spirit of the deceased wouldn't know which way to go, and would therefore go straight up, presumably to Heaven.

My heart would always be in my mouth, not knowing what scene of death and mutilation was waiting for us at the crash site. Because we often arrived just after the emergency services – or even at the same moment – the victims were often still trapped in their cage of bent and broken metal, their screams of agony cutting through an air that stank of spilled petrol, burnt rubber and blood.

I soon began to dread such duties. And because the office van was always driven at breakneck speed in order to quickly arrive at the crash scene, I became paranoid, convinced that we would also crash.

But little did I know that this neurosis was about to become reality.

On the night of Tuesday, November 5, 1968, I was marked down in the office diary to write a review of Barby Players' latest production, the title of which has long faded from my memory.

My colleague Martin Lawson had been assigned to cover a parish council meeting in a neighbouring village and it was arranged that he would pick me up in the office van. So off we went on our respective tasks that night as the sky around Rugby started to light up with the traditional flashes and minor explosions that yearly celebrate the demise of a certain Catholic terrorist back in 1605.

For all intents and purposes, it was just another routine night in the life of a couple of provincial newspaper reporters. But little did I know that my recurring fear was about to come true… I was about to become involved in a road accident myself.

Martin would have picked me up around 10pm and we were soon travelling along the narrow lanes that would eventually take us on to the main road back to Rugby and the *Advertiser* offices.

And it was then that Martin ran out of road. Mistaking an open farm gate for a continuation of the lanes, and realising his error too late, he brought the wheel round sharply.

But to no avail… the van flipped over and hit a tree. A third reporter, Keith Clarke, had been sitting in the passenger seat at the front, but I was perched on the spare wheel in the back.

As the van rolled over, I bounced about like a pea in a rattle, followed by the loose wheel, which came to a sickening crack of a rest on the lower part of my left leg, breaking both my shin bones.

What ensued was the worst pain I had ever endured. I would later learn that I had snapped my tibia and fibula bones, the latter splintering into two jagged shards.

All this information would later be established by an X-ray. But for now, all I could think about was that incessant, relentless pain. And it got worse. Much, much worse.

Meanwhile, Keith appeared to be unconscious, with his head resting on the dashboard. But Martin seemed to have escaped unscathed, and somehow, he managed to clamber out of the driver's seat.

Throwing open the van's rear doors, he must have realised from the noise I was making that I was badly hurt. Now, this was years before the advent of mobile phones, and for all he knew, we were miles from anywhere.

There was nothing for it but to hope that another vehicle would come along and he could flag the driver down.

One duly arrived, but with a callousness that astounds me to this day, the man said he couldn't stop and help as he was already late for work.

Thankfully, barely had his red tail lights vanished into the darkness than a second car appeared. And this time, the driver agreed to find a phone box and call the Hospital of St Cross which, as it happened, was not all that far away in Barby Road.

And so I began my long wait lying in the back of the van, wondering when the emergency services would arrive and release me from my torment, hopefully using painkillers to ease my condition.

Eventually, after what seemed to be an age, an ambulance finally arrived, and the crew freed me from my steel prison. After being lifted on to a stretcher in the back of the ambulance, I then endured the further ordeal of an agonisingly bumpy ride to the hospital.

Here I was seen by a surgeon who asked me whether I had consumed any alcohol that night. Thankfully on this occasion I had not – if that had been the case, then it would not have been possible to administer anaesthetic until the effects of the drink had worn off.

The surgeon then placed a mask over my face and told me to count from 10 to nought. I didn't get past nine.

At some stage during the early hours I regained consciousness in what appeared to be a men's prostate ward, judging by the number of transparent plastic bags and catheters at the side of each bed.

Eventually, despite the occasional agonised moans of my new companions, I slipped into a kind of half sleep, only to be awoken an hour or two later by a nurse.

She said that it was breakfast time and that after I'd eaten my meal, the physiotherapist would come round to see me and put me through a series of exercises.

Exercises? I was still in great pain, and protested that I wanted no such thing, but the matter was out of my hands. And lo and behold, not long after I'd finished the milk and cornflakes, along came the physio, who ordered me to sit on the side of the bed and hoist myself up on to the two wooden crutches she was holding.

Once again, my body was racked with pain as the force of gravity ensured that the weight of the plaster cruelly parted my shattered bones, only for them to rub together as I stood upright. It was mediaeval torture.

My protestations came to nothing. This was to be my road to recovery… but at the time it didn't seem much of an improvement on the road on which I had so recently come to grief.

That week's edition of the *Rugby Advertiser* carried a piece that recorded how one of its own journalists had actually made the news instead of reporting on it.

I would be out of action for several months but a system was soon developed whereby I worked from home and my typewritten copy was collected by van.

And who was driving that van? Yes, you've guessed. None other than Martin Lawson, my nemesis on that November the fifth night to remember, remember.

Learning the secret language

WE live in an age in which nearly everyone has access to a keyboard. The 'qwerty' layout is universally familiar to millions. But within my lifetime, the only people who could operate the typewriter were either predominantly female typists or journalists.

My first encounter with these machines came on the day I'd arrived at the *Rugby Advertiser*. And to begin with, it was very much a two-fingered affair.

More often than not, the keys locked together, and everything came to a stop as they had to be prised free of each other. Mistakes were many, and my early attempts at creating copy from village reports were patchy, to say the least.

Because of this, I was soon enrolled for night classes at the East Warwickshire College of Further Education. Here I would be acquainted with the art of touch typing on a Tuesday evening and with shorthand lessons on the Thursday.

To be honest, the touch typing never worked for me, mainly because I was 'two-finger' tapping during the day and the two styles were mutually incompatible.

I fared better with learning shorthand and was soon assimilating the short forms required if verbatim note-taking was eventually to be achieved. The shorthand lesson on Friday afternoons was also a useful 'top-up', although I never ever became highly skilled at using Isaac Pitman's celebrated system.

And unlike riding a bike, it's a case of use it or lose it. These days I would probably be sorely tested covering a court or council, which require a totally accurate note. There again, perhaps I'm being too hard on myself.

But as far as typing was concerned, I – like so many others – soon became proficient. So much so that I was able to take dictation whenever the Press Association news agency came on the phone with a story, as they did from time to time.

Most of the roles on a modern newspaper have been condensed and combined, one person being responsible for functions that were hitherto divided up among different categories of workers assigned to perform different tasks.

One such job was that of proof reader. Rows of readers would sit reading out loud the printed words, as other readers hovered with pen or pencil ready to pounce on any mistake that might emerge.

Errors were mainly missing words or 'typos', words with letters missing or transposed. Occasionally, the head reader – who was often a highly educated, erudite person – might spot an error of fact.

Head readers could be rather lofty individuals, sometimes having a working knowledge of Latin or even Greek, a great aid in not only knowing how to spell a given word, but also in identifying its linguistic origins. The importance of such 'roots' has been almost forgotten today.

When errors were found, they were marked with a proofing symbol. There were scores of these, the vast majority of which are probably no longer used.

The older editions of *The Writer's and Artist's Year Book* will give you some idea just how many symbols were in regular and daily use, once again a secret code known only to a few of the population.

Then there was the mysterious language known only to the 'hot metal' printer and journalist. For example, there was the 'orphan', a lone word at the end of a paragraph, and also the 'widow', a single word appearing at the top of a column of text. Both these were frowned upon by sub-editors and had to be overcome by introducing a word or words that would 'bump' the offender out of the way.

If a column dropped short, it had 'dog-legged', calling to mind the cocked leg of the male animal when it urinates. Continuing the canine theme, there was the 'dog's cock' or exclamation mark. Think about that one.

And in those days, every sub-editor and compositor had to know what was required if there was a note on a page layout for a 'mutton' or 'pica' rule underscore on a headline, a three-D box (three dimensional frame around a story), milled rule, stipple tint, nut each side (an 'en' indent space either side of a column) WOB (white on black reversed type) or a hanging indent.

In addition there was the drop cap (enlarged initial capital letter in the first paragraph of a story), ragged right text, crosshead, anchor piece, hamper, earpieces, masthead… and any number of terms for a trade that owed its origins to the 15th century and the inventions of William Caxton.

Like most human pursuits and endeavours, the world of journalists and printers was a closed shop to uninitiated outsiders. Little wonder then that printing in its heyday was at the top of the industrial tree, it secrets closely guarded.

In those days, the printers were at the front of the working class pecking order. And they knew it. Rookie journalists had to cotton on quickly to their ways, innate clannishness, and unchallengeable worship of the closed shop union system.

You crossed a printer at your peril. Fall out with one and you fell out with all of them. Be warned, my son.

I learnt this fairly quickly and treated them with respect, although never being afraid to fight my corner when all else had failed. The trick was to know whether a conflict situation required 'fight' or 'flight'.

Read it wrong and your life might well be made a misery for weeks or even months to come. But conversely, failure to stand up for yourself when necessary would give out the message that you were a soft touch. Being too reasonable or considerate had to be avoided at all costs… such behaviour could mark you out as being weak.

But in the main, I generally got on well with printers. There were always one of two with chips on their shoulders, as in other walks of life, and nothing you could do or say could change them.

But these were in the minority. And looking back, I think we had a mutual respect for one another.

Now, you will recall a character by the name of Derek Medlicott who made his appearance in an earlier chapter. Derek was a mountain of a man. He had an intimidating presence and his language on occasion would have made a squaddie blush.

Yet true to the cliché, he had the proverbial warm heart and was a man of great compassion. He and his wife had a disabled son whom Derek loved deeply. Even though I was still in my teens, I recognised that there were often many sides to people.

Derek rode a motorcycle and sidecar, in those days a cheap alternative to the motor car. One day, Len marked me down in the diary to do a job in Braunston, a large canalside village that lay between Rugby and Daventry.

My scooter was being repaired in a garage, so I told Len that I would have to travel by bus. By sheer chance, Derek overheard our conversation and promptly offered to give me a lift in his sidecar.

Len immediately agreed this was a good idea, and – without consulting me – told Derek that he could depart with his passenger forthwith.

My heart sank when I climbed into that sidecar. It was basically an old packing case made from chipboard. As I would soon discover to my cost, there was no suspension or anything to cushion the contact of this rickety contraption with the open road, save for a piece of crudely fitted foam mattress that looked for all the world like it had been chewed into shape by Derek's pet dog.

However, with great trepidation, I climbed into this mobile coffin. The Triumph Bonneville motorcycle roared into life… and soon we were bouncing and rattling through nearby Dunchurch and down the hill along the old London Road and into neighbouring Northamptonshire.

I've had a few bumpy and sometimes terrifying journeys down the years. But nothing gets near to that eight miles road trip to Braunston. I couldn't concentrate on the job either… all I could think about was the thought of the return trip to Rugby in Derek's infernal contraption.

But somehow or other, we arrived back at base in one piece. Once the throbbing Bonneville engine had been turned off, Derek turned to me and said: "Well, young John, wasn't that good? I bet you enjoyed that."

As the man said, there's no answer to that.

New brooms sweep all before them

BY early 1968, rock, folk and pop music was providing the soundtrack to my entire existence.

Not only that, but I had by now become very much a local personality, thanks to my weekly page in the *Advertiser*. I was being recognised everywhere I went and was revelling in my new-found fame.

Yes, I may have been a large fish in a small pond, but who cared? Everything was going swimmingly, if you'll pardon the pun.

There had also been a few changes at the paper. It had a new editor. David Briffett had taken over from John Lawson, who had been put out to grass in the summer of the previous year.

I was saddened and not a little shocked by his departure. He may have been rather 'old school' but his going had been abrupt and a surprise to most of us. As with all sudden change, it was a little destabilising.

In fact, I wrote a poem about this, likening his demise to that of an old, deceased Viking warrior being cast out into the ocean aboard a blazing longship. In a rare, unguarded moment of confessional candour, he told me how he no longer wished to be a newspaper editor "Judging by the way things were going in the provincial Press."

I got the impression he could see the growth of the looming tabloid revolution in regional newspapers and wanted no part of it.

David Briffett was a very different sort of editor. Aged only 29, he was typical of the new young blood that was then rising through the ranks of the industry.

The 1960s were in full swing and young men and women from all classes and walks of life were now getting jobs in the media, reflecting how the world of music, film and theatre was changing, thanks to all the raw talent now flooding in from all over Britain.

David valued my page and seemed to want to make it a focal part of the paper. As if to emphasise the point, he renamed it *The John Phillpott Feature*. Thrilled that I should have been granted such prominence, I determined not to let him down.

Before long, I was out on the town most nights, going to gigs, theatres and pubs. I was continually chasing stories, chatting to contacts, picking up pieces of gossip, rumours… absolutely anything could and did make copy for my page.

By the time I was aged 19, I had become a personality, the voice of young Rugby. Immodest this may seem, but it was true.

And this was indeed a time for youth. The 1960s had only really got going after the Profumo affair brought shame and a permanent collapse in respect by the general public for the ruling elite.

The immediate period after the Second World War may have started this process but there is no doubt that this sea change accelerated in that momentous second decade after the six years of conflict.

Then there had been the advent of The Beatles, Rolling Stones and numerous other groups that combined to form the 'British Invasion' of America, when our friends across the ocean were momentarily taken by surprise as the old Mother Country Britannia once again ruled the waves.

David Briffett may have looked 'square' on account of his well-groomed hair and immaculate suits, but there was no doubt about it. He represented the new, whereas Len Archer and Geoff Ambler were very much yesterday's men.

Yes, this may seem like I'm being unduly harsh about two undoubtedly fine journalists who had served the *Advertiser* well. But symptomatic of a growing void was the fact that while they thought most young people were little more than wasters and long-haired layabouts, David Briffett regarded them as being tomorrow's readers of the paper. And therein lay the difference. Briffett was a man of vision.

He was certainly no radical in the political sense. But he could see that society was changing. And if anything personified these many upheavals it had probably been the release of The Beatles' *Sgt Pepper's Lonely Hearts Club Band* during 1967, the Summer of Love. And this is how I remember it…

Don Eales came swaggering down Sheep Street, his Greek god's mane of hair shining like spun gold in the spring sunshine. I was so jealous – this was 1967, and although the fabled summer of love had hardly got much beyond foreplay, a hippy hairstyle certainly gave its owner a head start when it came to impressing the girls.

How could my lanky old Small Faces centre-parting job compete with his Inca headdress of a thatch? Somehow though, I gained the distinct impression that our respective coiffures were not to be the main subject on the agenda that day…

Squinting over his John Lennon spectacles, he had caught sight of my kaftan-clad outline – I was off-duty and could wear what I liked – and crossed over the road, punching the air as he approached. Don was almost speechless, struggling to get his words out.

"Hey John, it's out at last – and what a monster! Come on, let's pop into the Co-op and get Bob Hillyard to play us a few tracks!"

By that he meant an alcove called the Disc Cabin at the Co-operative Stores in Chapel Street, Rugby. And yes, we all knew Bob, an expert on all kinds of music, especially rhythm and blues… but what was Don on about?

"The new Beatles album, stupid!" said Don, as he grabbed my sleeve and frog-marched me past the Il Cadore coffee bar and then down the steps of the Co-op into the Disc Cabin where the owlish Bob was busy sorting through a pile of 45s.

Bob heard our approach and turned, his face giving only the slightest signs of recognition. He was immaculately suited and booted, his mod finery neatly topped off by a tab-collar shirt with knitted tie woven into the tiniest of knots. Yes, Bob was the Biz.

"So you want to hear it then," said Bob, jamming a Bristol tipped into his mouth. "Let me tell you something," he wheezed, exhaling blue smoke in our direction. "This is going to be one of the greatest records of all time. They've called it *Sgt Pepper's Lonely Hearts Club Band…*"

There are a number of events in our post-war culture that define our existence. It is said that President John Kennedy's death acts as a time frame for all those who were around at the time – and the same probably applies to all those baby boomers who can pinpoint exactly where they were on that early June morning almost six decades ago.

It was 20 years ago today, Sergeant Pepper taught the band to play… no, no. Can it really be an astonishing almost 60 years since John Lennon and Paul McCartney penned the masterpiece that would ensure pop music would never ever be the same again?

For weeks, the music press had been printing stories hinting of some great work being hatched at London's Abbey Road Studios. Publications such as *New Musical Express* and *Melody Maker* had carried story after story.

The Beatles had been spotted coming and going for weeks – Paul McCartney, in particular, had been repeatedly door-stepped by Fleet Street journalists, asking the usual crass questions that passed for pop reporting in those impossibly far-off days.

And then it arrived. Up and down Britain, brown cardboard boxes packed with the new album appeared outside record stores. It would prove to be one of the most distinctive long players of all time, the much-celebrated montage of famous faces giving way to a vermilion wash on the inner and outer folding sleeve.

Within days, the nation's youth were falling over themselves to name the celebrities featured on the cover, like some huge identity parade. There's Marilyn Monroe, Bob Dylan... and wow, there must be something really weird about this album if Aleister Crowley's been included...

Copies were bought up as soon as they were delivered, shops often running out as suppliers struggled to keep pace with demand. Soon, everyone had a favourite track, a song with lyrics that seemed to apply to them on some intimate level. It was as if The Beatles were talking directly to the listener.

Getting Better... so many of us had messed about at school. *Within You Without You*... those recently converted to transcendental meditation knew precisely what George Harrison was saying.

And then there was *A Day in The Life*... guitarist John Lennon's piece of mystical 60s musical reportage that hinted so darkly at recent real-life events.

But it was not just the music that was different from anything else that had been heard before. Inside the album were pop-up characters, including the mysterious Sergeant Pepper himself.

In years to come, proud owners would rue the day they had discarded those pieces of coloured cardboard – mint-condition copies of the record were destined to become extremely valuable, but only if the pop-ups had survived. Predictably, mine were soon lost or thrown away as being of no consequence.

Then there were the garbled words at the end of side two. Everyone came up with a different interpretation, many saying that Paul McCartney was sending out some coded message to humanity.

This was a world searching for meaning – in those heady days anything said by the moptop pop prince was instantly absorbed, like raindrops falling on sun-parched desert sands.

Bob Hillyard eased the shiny vinyl out of its paper and polythene inner sleeve. The simply designed Parlophone logo on a black background appeared so basic, giving no clue whatsoever to the treasures that lay buried in those gleaming grooves.

At a glance, this appeared to be no different from the other Beatle masterpieces. And in any event, how were the Fabs going to follow something as exquisitely perfect as their previous album *Revolver?* The needle fell upon the spinning disc, there was just the hint of that telltale bacon and eggs crackle... and then it happened.

"It was 20 years ago today, Sergeant Pepper taught the band to play..."

Incredibly, it's almost three times that now. But despite the passage of all this time, I will never forget that sunny day in June, 1967, when my pal Don

Eales stopped me in the street and broke the news that a certain military gentleman was parading his musical troops… and ready to march into pop history.

The release of *Sgt Pepper* was a watershed, not just in popular culture, but throughout society as a whole. Suddenly, it became all right, indeed respectable, to like pop music.

Before *Sgt Pepper*, pop had been merely a working class distraction, an opiate for the masses, definitely not for the intelligentsia. Besides, 'intelligent' young people – the minority that went to university in those days – liked traditional jazz.

Now the latter were queuing up to discuss on the loftiest intellectual levels the meanings that lurked within those black vinyl grooves.

Not just that, but journalists on the quality broadsheets were also starting to fall over one another in the rush to admit the four Scousers into the hallowed halls of high culture.

And all the while, classical music experts were waxing lyrical about cadences, scales, progressions and modulations, likening Lennon and McCartney to the great composers of the 19th century.

This was not just 'beat' music my friends… oh no, surely not, this is art!

This then were just some of the many changes occurring across British society at that time. And in an admittedly very small way, I was busy reflecting, through a small provincial newspaper, the seismic changes that were now shaking post war Britain to its very core.

Dancing to a different tune

WHEN David Briffett became editor of the *Advertiser,* quite a few of the former working habits hit the proverbial spike.

No longer were reporters required to take names at fetes, budgerigar and rabbit shows, or cover funerals – unless the deceased had been a prominent person.

Instead, reporters would be sent to events and, rather make lists, were to keep their eyes peeled for the off-diary story. Suddenly, almost overnight, much of the daily drudgery fell away.

The story behind the story started to reveal itself and acquire a new importance, no longer to be smothered in an ocean of names, all set in six point type and advancing like packed masses of typographical infantry across the broadsheet page.

Soon, human interest stories were appearing in the *Advertiser's* columns, aided by a much slicker and navigable design, thanks to David Briffett and a talented sub-editor by the name of Pat Armstrong.

Pat was a no-nonsense pragmatist from Tamworth, Staffordshire. Although he would outwardly give the impression of being totally laid-back, he would occasionally clash with David Briffett, always standing his corner.

Like so many provincial journalists in those days, Pat was a skilled all-rounder who could perform all the tasks of the trade, whether it was writing, sub-editing or planning a page layout.

He played a major role in presenting the *Advertiser* to the public as a well-designed, attractive product... a very different paper from the one created by the more cautious and conservative John Lawson.

The paper in those days was well staffed, in stark contrast to the low numbers of employees in the modern newspaper office. In addition to the editor and his deputy, there was a sub-editor, sports editor and deputy, chief reporter and deputy plus several general reporters.

The paper's circulation back then was in excess of 36,000 copies a week, a figure of dizzying magnitude when compared to the puny numbers achieved nowadays.

One undoubted reason for this healthy situation was because papers covered absolutely everything. So there was a lot of content for the customer, something for everyone.

Reporters generally regarded their calling as not so much a job more a way of life. Once that night job was finished, we'd meet in either the pub, or take a few bottles back to the office.

If it was a case of the pub, then the watering hole of choice would be either the London House or the Black Swan, known affectionately, if a little predictably, as 'the Dirty Duck'.

The quality of beer was going downhill rapidly by the late 1960s, thanks to the demise of smaller breweries and the advent of sterile, carbonated beer, the result of industrial-style production.

Much of this tepid slop had little resemblance to what we had once known, but thankfully, both our favourite pubs seemed to have resisted much of this change.

Birmingham-brewed Ansells was popular in this part of the Midlands, the beer retaining the qualities that were at this time fast vanishing from many people's locals. Soon, the hand-pulled pint became a rarity.

The Black Swan, Chapel Street.

Nevertheless, there were a few oases of real ale, such as the Avon Mill pub at the bottom of Newbold Road. This hostelry was run by an old woman, whose name is now sadly lost to the march of time – I just recall she was called 'Ma' by all the regulars.

She would undoubtedly have been one of the longest-serving licensees in the Rugby area, that much I do know.

The Avon Mill served Joules Ales, a particularly tasty, hoppy and malty brew. I remember calling in one day with Guy Edgson and sinking quite a few pints between us. No doubt it was all in the interest of 'work' and following up a story.

If we returned to the office equipped with a few bottles, then the guitars – which were stored in a disused backroom at the *Advertiser* – would come out, and we'd strum away for an hour or two, playing mainly Buddy Holly tunes or the few folk songs we could muster between us.

Apart from the musical instruments, the room was virtually bare save for a battered table, some equally dilapidated chairs… and a mattress.

Why a mattress? Well because from time to time, one of us might stay in the offices overnight, especially if there was an early start in the morning or there had been a heavy session the night before.

All this might seem as if we were a gang of literary tramps, rough sleepers even, and to some extent that exactly what we were. But you have to understand that ours was an unorthodox way of life, far removed from the workaday reality of most people.

Journalists in those days tended to be highly individualistic, a few of them most definitely misfits. Other than busking or begging on the streets, there was little prospect of us succeeding in any working environment other than a newspaper office.

This reality very much worked for me. Even though the magic words 'grammar school' still opened employers' doors, there were still no guarantees, especially if you only had a handful of 'o' levels.

But here I was in a job, unlike many of my former classmates who had either gone into the sixth form, college, or – in just a few cases – seriously astray.

Everyone was 'streamed' by the education system. Throughout my time at Lawrence Sheriff, I had been in the lower form for my year, basically a dumping ground for the less successful and more difficult boys.

Such labelling was unfair. Many of the boys in my form were, despite being slightly unruly, highly intelligent and creative people, some of whom would go on to have rewarding, if slightly unorthodox, careers.

I don't do false modesty and that's why I would include myself as being a member of this dubious band of brothers. There's no doubt that I could sometimes be quite a wild young man, but I was also someone unafraid to stand their ground when required, and to challenge authority if necessary. In some ways, these traits helped to equip me for the job.

The main reason why night jobs were always written up that same evening was because of the widespread newspaper maxim that reporters should always start every day with an 'empty' notebook.

It was a serious offence to go into the office the morning after a night job with copy still to write up.

All these type-written stories had to be dropped into Len's in-tray. Every morning he would arrive with a resounding crash through the reporters' room door, hang up his Harold Wilson-style Gannex raincoat, order me to make him a cup of tea… and then he'd start sifting through the pieces created the night before.

Occasionally, his bright blue-eyed gaze would alight on me, not always something that I welcomed. He might ask me a question to which I invariably had no answer.

To be fair, he was only doing his job, but there was often a marked fierceness in his voice that usually prefaced a telling-off.

The fact that he had a very loud voice and a chronic stutter didn't help matters, either. But there again, part of the problem was me and my bolshie nature. Len probably wasn't that much different to many of the chief reporters and news editors around in those days.

I was but a callow youth and there's no doubt I had to be licked into shape. And perhaps Len was the man to do it. I have long accepted this was a job that had to be done.

However, Len could be engaging and entertaining company once we were down the pub. He was unstintingly generous and good-hearted when the mood took him, especially when he'd had the first few beers of the day.

Len was also receptive to amusing stories and would laugh like a drain if one really took his fancy. Despite a tendency to be overbearing, he did indeed have some good points. I soon learnt how to entertain and make him laugh, usually by what is universally known as 'acting daft'.

On reflection, it would probably have worked better had I been a bit older when I started on the *Advertiser*. Sixteen was a very young age to start work in the febrile atmosphere of a newspaper office.

I was a teenager and had a lot of the bad attitudes common to the condition. As a result, he often treated me like a naughty schoolboy who had to be knocked into shape, beaten into line.

That's why he was always on at me regarding my clothes or hairstyle. I accept that now… it's just that I didn't back then. And, for what it's worth, I forgive him.

Yet sometimes, when I look back at the few monochrome photographs taken of me at that time, I do wonder what all the fuss was about. Smart jacket, white shirt and tie, hair centre-parted but not all that long taking into account the era… maybe it was all a sign of the changes then engulfing the country.

Britain was still dragging itself out of the drab, grey 1950s, a period of flat caps, faded demob suits and the obligatory gaberdine macs needed to protect against the constant rain that seems to be either present or threatening in all the old photographs of the time.

Eventually the old order would be beaten down by the sheer force of change, a tidal wave of new thinking that would progressively gather pace until nothing on Earth could stop it.

And although he almost certainly didn't recognise it at the time, new editor David Briffett was playing his part in adding to the momentum that would soon sweep away the old and usher in the new.

Len died a few years ago in a nursing home in Daventry. The years inexorably pass by, but I often think about him and those long-lost days on the *Rugby Advertiser* back in Albert Street during the 1960s. And I hope he's resting in peace, yes I really do.

Batman and Boy Blunder

IT is a lingering, nagging fear that will probably stay with me until my dying day.

This is the reason why I still scrutinise all written work with an obsessive eye, not just reading the words, but also digesting the letters with a hunter's tenacity, running to ground any mistake that might be lurking.

I must have written millions of words down the years. And although the thought bothers me, there will indeed have been mistakes that have got through my defences and found their way onto the printed page.

It's said in publishing circles that a book of average length should contain no more that three or four errors. This is probably because it's accepted that mere mortals will always make mistakes, regardless of the amount of care that's been taken.

If there's one thing that was dinned into me during my early days as a journalist then it was the need to 'get it right'. These days, you can see any amount of carelessness, sloppiness, bad grammar and poor command of the English tongue, thanks to social media.

Technology has allowed the illiterate to present their musings to a captive audience on a daily basis. Once, no one would be aware of such people's capacity to mangle the language of Shakespeare. Now it is on a million screens, both large and small, for the entire world to see.

News reporting – unlike feature writing or comment pieces – may not have been an exact science but there were a number of rules that were sacrosanct. You broke them at your peril.

By far the most important was the need for complete accuracy. It was of paramount importance. Copy had to be 'clean' – not littered with over-typed words or pencilled crossings-out – and neatly presented in short paragraphs, with the introductory sentence by itself on a single page to facilitate the writing of the sub-editor's instructions.

This was called 'the intro' and the convention was that it should not normally contain more than 25 to 30 words.

The first paragraph of a story was often set in a larger type size. This meant that intros were usually allowed to gather en masse in a separate copy tray. Once they had been set by the printer, they would later be added to the stories to which they belonged.

All production journalists had once been reporters themselves, so a degree of leniency was usually extended to hacks that were a bit messier or wordy than others. It didn't stop the moans, though.

Nevertheless, some habitually careless reporters acquired bad reputations and were sometimes shouted at by exasperated sub-editors. This wouldn't happen these days, thanks to political correctness.

And it was not unknown for 'old school' editors to reject poorly-presented copy with a brusque "Go and type this up again… and neatly, please!" When this happened, lessons were quickly learnt. It was the same with unsatisfactorily written headlines, which could be unceremoniously thrown back to be rewritten by their creators.

All the same, reporters' typing skills varied according to the prowess or dedication of the individual. Most trainees got the hang of it pounding away on an old Remington. I got up to speed quite soon, and was able to take dictated copy over the phone when the need arose.

Then, as now, the London-based Press Association (PA) supplied British newspapers with stories from far and near if they were of local interest. Once the caller had identified themselves as being a PA journalist, on went the headphones and off you went. Occasionally, you had to contend with a bad-tempered person on the other end who was not all that impressed with your typing rate of knots.

But that was the exception. And most PA journalists were, in the main, genial sorts who were just trying to do a job like you.

When a story had been typed up, it was normal practice to use carbon paper to ensure you had a duplicate copy, basically a case of 'belt and braces.' Absolutely anything can get lost or mislaid and typewritten copy was most certainly no exception.

When a piece of written material was of no longer use, it was 'spiked'. The spike was literally that – a sharpened, metal skewer in a circular wooden stand. These days 'spike' means something quite different.

If something was 'spiked' it had, for all intents and purposes, been thrown away. Except that it hadn't really. And that was because that spike was your insurance if the original copy had been mislaid, or there had been a complaint from a member of the public about a story, and the facts had to be checked.

Today, 'memory' is stored in computers with all created material automatically being backed-up. But years ago, every single item of recorded knowledge would end up being pierced by a miniature harpoon emerging from a small piece of polished wood.

But it worked just as well… although you always had to take care not to spear the palm of your hand in the process.

In newspapers up and down the land, then – as now – accuracy was the order of the day. As a famous editor once observed, comment might indeed be free, but facts were sacred.

Every Friday in weekly newspaper offices up and down the land, the editorial staff waited in trepidation for the phone to ring, knowing only too well that there was the distinct possibility that it would be a member of the public with a complaint to make.

Like 1940 Battle of Britain fighter pilots sprawled on the grass waiting for the order to 'scramble', those of us not assigned court reporting duties readied ourselves for the first call to come in.

When it finally happened, more often that not it might be a trifling moan about something in the paper that the caller simply didn't like, rather than a complaint about an alleged error of fact.

Once, I transposed the names of some class winners in a report of the Rugby and District Chrysanthemum and Dahlia Society's annual autumn show. That was it. A good telling-off loomed on the horizon…

A certain L E Steane not only expressed his displeasure to a mere mortal in the reporters' room, but also took the matter further by contacting the editor who was – and wouldn't you just know it – a personal friend.

I was called in to Mr Lawson's office and given a real roasting, the first of several that I would receive. Golden rule number one… if you are going to make a mistake, make sure it's not about someone who's a friend of the editor.

On another occasion, I managed a hat-trick of blunders, the famous three in a row. None of them was all that earth-shattering, but it was enough to make Mr Lawson warn me that my days on the *Advertiser* could well be numbered if I carried on like this.

"I won't be able to keep you John Phillpott," he said, without a hint of malice in his voice. Just a matter-of-fact 'shape up or you'll be shipped out if you don't up your game'.

This roasting had come not long before my six-month probationary period was up and understandably shook me to the core. After that, although

I would continue to make the occasional mistake, never again did I manage to perpetrate such a catalogue of catastrophes.

But there was just one, enormous mega-blunder that, unknown to me, lay just around the corner… as if waiting in ambush. A month or two after signing my indentures, I was sent to report on a speech by Sir Jack Scamp, a man who was then known across the Midlands as the car industry's 'trouble shooter'.

I've got to be honest here. I was still aged only 16, and not only hadn't got a clue about the issues, but also didn't understand anything he was saying. As a result I seriously misreported his speech.

Amazingly, I didn't receive a telling-off. I think the deputy editor and Len Archer realised that I had been completely out of my depth and actually should never have been sent on such a complicated and difficult reporting mission.

But once again this was a salutary lesson to check and double check copy, and also rammed home the need for me to do my homework properly before leaving the office on an assignment.

From then on, my new maxim was never go out at half-cock, and if in doubt, leave out. And these were the words that rang in my head and helped guide me through the next few years of my life as a provincial newspaper reporter.

Lure of the open road

REPORTERS these days tend to be mainly deskbound. Newspapers have drastically cut back on staff in recent years and the old tried and tested methods of walking the streets, spending time in pubs, studying notice boards and generally keeping track of the public's doings have all but vanished.

News desks can no longer afford to send a reporter out on his or her travels on the off-chance that a story might be uncovered. The old command of "Don't come back to the office until you've got a story in your notebook" has been lost in the mists of time.

Yes, there are still meetings to cover. But today's reporters are required to stay at their desks so that they can supply an endless stream of copy gleaned from press releases, handouts and council minutes.

The vast majority of interviews are now conducted on the phone, whereas once, the opposite was not only the case, but the cast-iron rule.

Never do on the phone something that is better achieved by meeting and talking to the person concerned. These days, the face-to-face encounter is the exception rather than the rule.

To give you some idea of how much face-to-face contact with the public was highly prized, let me give you this example. One of my jobs as show page writer was to visit the main four shops that sold records in Rugby town centre and pick up lists of that week's top ten chart hits.

As far as three of the outlets were concerned, it was a case of straight in, pick up the list, and then out again. Not so in the case of Disci in the High Street, however.

And that was because the chap behind the counter was my old school friend, Brian Meredith. Brian was not only drummer with local band The Big Idea but also someone with an encyclopaedic knowledge of classics, pop, jazz, soul and blues.

He would often put several singles behind the counter in readiness for my weekly visit, usually a Wednesday. I'd walk into the shop, and after the usual greeting, he might say something like: "Hey John, I've got something you're going to love. It's called *I Gotcha* by Joe Tex. Just listen to that funky drum intro!"

It will not surprise you when I say that my return to the office on Wednesdays was often, to say the least, slightly delayed. Such a scenario these days would be inconceivable.

The enforced isolation of the present-day reporter from the target audience is just one of many reasons why provincial newspapers are in managed decline. And to get even more of an idea of how journalists once spent much of their time 'on the road' you can take this as a further example.

One day, Len Archer received a tip-off that a person had been hit and killed by a train on the railway line between Rugby and Coventry. He lost no time in ordering me to go with him and deputy chief reporter Guy Edgson to try and find the site of the tragedy.

To this day, I cannot for the life of me see what this would have achieved, but this was typical of the journalistic mentality of those days. Get out of the office, get the story… and rush back to write it up. And then get out of the office again…

Here's another example. In the spring of 1968, a headless body had been discovered on the London to Carlisle line, which came through Rugby. The town, incidentally, had once hosted the biggest railway junction in Britain, bigger even than that of Swindon in Wiltshire.

There was absolutely no suggestion whatsoever that the murder had any links to our patch. But this made no difference at all. Len led a team of us down to Rugby Midland Station in order to interview as many passengers as we could.

Most of those we spoke to were amazed when we asked them if they knew anything about a murder. Had they seen anything… and where?

However, one old woman – in true Dame Margaret Rutherford style – beat Len soundly over the head with her umbrella, while screaming at the top of her voice: "Murder? *Murder!*"

Talk about the occupational hazards of the job… and while it was perhaps painful for Len it certainly proved highly amusing for the rest of us.

I worked on the *Advertiser* for more than four years and have to admit that a fair proportion of that time was spent in public houses. As I've related in a previous chapter, I met all sort of characters in my travels around north Warwickshire and the adjoining counties, many of them decent and ordinary hard-working folk.

But I also came into contact with members of the local criminal fraternity. Some of these villains were highly manipulative and could easily draw you into their murky world if you let them.

An old school friend of mine was lured into what turned out to be a break-in at Rugby School. My friend only just managed to extricate himself in time, realising the nature of their game.

The plaque to William Webb Ellis at Rugby School.

Most of these people were petty criminals and, as far as I know, never entered the 'big time'. In any event, I doubt very much whether the bigger fish in nearby Coventry, Leicester and Birmingham would have admitted such small fry into their midst.

None of these individuals seemed to hold down regular jobs. They could always be found propping up the bar at the London House, 'Dirty Duck' or eating hamburgers and chips at the Il Cadore coffee bar in Chapel Street. I daresay some of them are still there, although certainly not at the Il Cadore, which was demolished a number of years ago.

I knew them all. And while I acknowledged their presence, nevertheless always gave them a fairly wide berth. They were losers and definitely bad news. There was no way that I wanted to get too close to them. There was just too much at stake. My job, for a start.

I doubt very much whether reporters on provincial newspapers these days come into contact with so many dodgy characters in the way that I did back then.

Another reason why today's trainees don't tend to meet such a wide range of people is because new recruits tend to be almost exclusively graduates, middle-class youngsters from good homes.

I was aged only 16 when I started work and was an impressionable lad with no experience of life and the wider world. All I knew about was the small village in which I had grown up.

Young people joining the industry today will be in their early 20s, college or university educated, and far removed from the frenetic teenage world of the 1960s.

All the bad influences and angst-soaked turmoil of the formative years will have been left behind. This was not the case as far as I was concerned, being disadvantaged in the sense that there was no time for me to make a steady transition from school to work.

It was difficult to shake free from some former associates, many of whom wanted to drag you down into the hole they were happy to occupy. By the time I had left the *Rugby Advertiser* in the autumn of 1969, my social life had thankfully levelled out.

By that time, I had created a niche for myself, not only as a respected chronicler of Rugby's life and times, but as a budding personality about town, being invited to numerous events purely because of who I was.

That year would see me involved in one of the highlights in Rugby's social diary, the town's 'Rag Week' celebrations.

This had been started years before by the BTH apprentices and featured, among other things, a carnival procession through the town and the Rag Ball, a dance which had, by the early 60s started to feature 'beat' groups instead of the more staid dance bands that had really been a hangover from the 1930s and 40s.

The Rag Ball was either held at the Drill Hall in Bridget Street or the Benn Memorial Hall, a venue that would go on to host some of the top rock and pop acts of those days.

As part of Rag Week, I organised a 'beauty contest' – now considered very politically incorrect – followed by a ball, which I went on to compere on the big night when the winner was announced.

Every week, the *Advertiser* printed photographs and short biographies of the contestants. There was a huge build-up to the final, which was judged by a number of local luminaries including the then Labour MP for Rugby, Bill Price.

He was a real man of the people, on the centre ground of the Labour Party, and extremely popular in Rugby among voters of all persuasions. He was also a journalist and naturally sought the company of local reporters such as myself.

Occasionally, we would all pile over to his home in the village of Frankton, near Rugby, for union meetings that were always followed by serious drinking sessions at the local pub.

I've talked to many people who were young during the 1960s and they virtually all agree that there was a definite vibrancy to that decade that is singularly lacking these days.

In an era before the internet, social media, tweets and so forth, people not only talked to each other, they also took more interest in what was happening across wider society.

Rugby's Rag Week that summer was, as in previous years, a great success and I'm glad to have played my part.

But one night my growing conceit almost landed me in real trouble. I'd had a few beers in local hostelries and was walking along the town's Hillmorton Road when I was accosted by two plainclothes policemen.

Their manner was extremely brusque and this annoyed me, my irritation no doubt increased by that night's alcoholic intake. I was ordered to identify myself as 'there had been a burglary' and foolishly I started to give them plenty of 'lip'.

This was a big mistake. They then threatened to beat me up. Even more stupidly, I said they could try their luck but they were dealing with none other than 'John Phillpott of the *Advertiser*'. So you can see, I thought very highly of myself indeed. Especially after several drinks.

"Oh, Phillpott, is it?" said one. "We might have known!" And then they were gone, almost as quickly as they had arrived.

The next day, I told David Briffett about the encounter and decided to complain to the Chief Constable of Warwickshire. A week or two later, his deputy arrived at the office to interview me. It was not long before he bluntly announced that the officers concerned had no recollection of the alleged exchange in Hillmorton Road.

And that would have been that... had it not been for a tip-off in a dance hall from a friend who said that the two policemen were hatching a plot to plant drugs on me. I was to be 'fitted up' for possession of cannabis, then a serious charge that carried a prison sentence.

It all came to nothing. But from then on, I started to become more cautious and less full of my own importance. My out-of-control, vastly overblown ego was potentially leading me into stormy seas... and there was now an urgent need for some plain sailing into much calmer waters.

Just give me that rock and roll music

BY the spring of 1968, I was probably the best known young person in Rugby. Yes, that does sound impossibly pompous and self-regarding, but the facts of the matter are that this was palpably true.

I wrote an entire broadsheet page every week, packed with news and gossip, and my fame – although extending to no more than a 15-mile radius – started to generate prestigious invitations.

And that's how I came to be involved in what would go down in rock 'n' roll history as one of the first major pop festivals to be held in the British provinces.

The eventual line-up was truly staggering. We have for many years lived in a world of rock music played in gigantic stadiums, with light shows and pyrotechnics that seem to get ever more dramatic and lavish.

Over time, fans have become used to extortionate ticket prices and rip-off prices for food, drink and merchandise. Rock music has become corporate, bloated with its own importance, product for the masses.

Once, it was the voice of protest. But these days, it is the throaty roar of bullish capitalism, over-driven guitars replacing the sound of machines in those dark satanic mills of yesteryear.

Desperately hip young men and women wear the ragged robes of weekend dissent while donning the mantle of money. Rock 'n' roll, once an underground movement, the sound of streets or fields, is now the echoes of a billion cash registers.

It is blended and mixed by technicians who sell a uniform drug to successive, unquestioning generations who are fast losing all respect for the now aging trailblazers who made it all possible in the first place.

Rarely do you see in mainstream media any paying of respect or acknowledgement to the hard work and occasional sacrifices made by my generation in the 1960s.

We're the ones who weathered the storms of parental and Establishment disapproval, the ones who took the brickbats and endured the constant ridicule of our then elders and 'betters'.

Nevertheless, we must return to the spring and summer of 1969, times of even greater changes than those that had gone before, not all of it good. For this was the year that Rolling Stones founder Brian Jones died in the swimming pool at his home Cotchford Farm, Sussex.

There is now general acceptance that Jones was killed, either deliberately or as a result of horseplay that had got out of hand in the pool. No one knew this at the time and the assumption – for that is what it was – had been that Jones had gone for a midnight swim under the influence of drink, drugs or both. It was Brian Jones we're talking about, after all.

Brian Jones had been a massive influence on my life ever since the advent of The Stones as a recording band in the summer of 1963. I had been captivated by the lantern-jawed young musician who looked like a schoolgirl yet played the guitar and diatonic harmonica like a black bluesman from the Mississippi Delta.

So great was his influence that within a week of seeing the group onstage at Rugby's Granada cinema I had paid a local music shop a visit and bought the same type of harmonica – or 'blues harp' as they soon became known – as played by my blond-haired reprobate of a hero.

As each day passed, The Stones rolled relentlessly on, gathering fame. And there was soon plenty of opportunity to see Brian Jones on the small screen, his chalk-white face leering out of the black and white television set, a golden dome of hair and perfect set of gleaming teeth transfixing or infuriating, depending on the age of the viewer.

In fact, back in the 1960s, most parents made no secret of their thoughts. Just look at him, he's like a girl. *They want to put blokes like that in the Army… that would knock some sense into him.*

But he was my role model. With the countenance of an angel and the morals of an alley cat, the blues-mad boy from Hatherley, near Cheltenham, touched the lives of many a baby boomer boy who hankered after a slice of that early 1960s rock action.

And I was one of them. For by the age of 15, I had become obsessed with The Stones, and in particular, their androgynous tunesmith. Jones was the undisputed pied piper for a generation of youths who dreamed that they also might find success chopping guitar chords or wailing the blues on a cheap harmonica.

Jones was primarily a jazz player. Most of the young men who made up the British Invasion that took America by storm in the 1960s were beat group musicians. They were influenced by black R&B pioneers, but mainly produced a more sanitised version of the originals.

However, Jones was different – his no-nonsense, gutsy approach sounded completely authentic. This further added to the mystery, for the music he played was obviously masculine – yet he looked like a woman! He was part man, part god – and that's undoubtedly why we all worshipped him.

For boys of my age, homage was usually paid in front of the wardrobe mirror. Locked away in our bedroom dens, countless numbers of adolescent boys like me posed with hair scraped forward, clad in tight jeans and Cuban-heeled boots, wielding imaginary guitars.

In my case it was a 30 shilling instrument with two strings missing. I would spend hours playing the Stones' first LP on a green Dansette record player, miming along to *Walking the Dog, Carol, I'm A King Bee* or *Route 66.*

Periodically, I would be caught in the act of imaginary stardom by my father, bursting into the bedroom insisting that I "turned off that blooming jungle music". The obsession was further intensified after I saw the Rolling Stones at the Rugby Granada Theatre early in 1964.

It's not difficult to understand what a shock all this must have been for our parents. Only 20 years before, they were suffering Adolf Hitler's blitzkrieg that had rained down bombs and bereavement.

What WAS happening to British youth – were these the young people for whom a generation had fought and died?

Meanwhile, schoolmasters used scorn and humiliation to fight the creeping hairy menace, or just resorted to time-honoured methods such as tweaking pubescent sideboards that they decided had crept too far down the jaw.

But it just got worse. As the 1960s wore on, hair grew longer and longer, openly mocking the short-back-and-sides generation that increasingly shook a collective head in exasperation at the apparent breakdown of everything society had once stood for.

Elsewhere, Establishment figures quietly sought some accommodation with the new young Bohemians. Fellow Rolling Stones Mick Jagger and Keith Richards had been found guilty of drugs offences in the summer of 1967 and the severity of their sentence was famously challenged by *The Times* leader article headlined 'Who breaks a butterfly on a wheel?'

Jones was that butterfly. He was found dead in the swimming pool at his house – once the home of writer A A Milne – on the night of July 2-3, 1969. For many of us, this was the day the music died.

For if the early rockers will always remember that day in February, 1959, when Buddy Holly was killed, then our tragedy was the premature death of the fast-burning star who had shone all-too briefly and brought a light into our lives that still – arguably – shines today.

Two days after Jones died, the Rolling Stones played their famous gig in Hyde Park, London, perhaps one of the greatest rock events in history. This was undoubtedly an ordeal for them, because they had sacked Jones from the band a few weeks before… and now he was dead.

This was a show that I simply couldn't afford to miss and so I caught the train to London on the morning of Saturday, July 5, 1969. Compere Sam Cutler would later memorably dub them 'the greatest rock 'n' roll band in the world'. There is no doubt that he was right, because the world of rock music changed forever on that boiling hot day in 1969.

And I'll never forget how it all started to unfold that hot afternoon when I saw the billboards for the *Coventry Evening Telegraph*. 'Pop star found dead in swimming pool' they screamed, the fat black type announcing the demise of Rolling Stones bad boy Brian Jones.

The guitarist with the golden mop, the young man who had a world of teenage girls at his feet, was gone. And with only two days to go before the band's concert in Hyde Park, what would happen now?

Jones may have been forced out of the band a few weeks earlier, but the great fear was the possibility of cancellation. It might also mean a couple of reporters on the *Rugby Advertiser* would be extremely disappointed.

This was the closing year of that momentous decade. I was aged 20 and my sidekick, Chris Poole, was a year younger. We had managed to convince the concert organisers – Blackhill Enterprises – that the *Advertiser* needed to cover the event. As if… But our barefaced cheek had paid off. For after a few telephone calls, two sky blue tickets for the Press enclosure arrived in the post.

Chris was the main mover here, for he had struck up a friendship with concert promoter Sam Cutler, the man who would not only oversee the historic London gig, but also go on to become the Stones chief road manager.

In fact, he was present a few months later at the infamous Altamount, California, racing stadium concert in which a young black man was beaten to death by Hells Angels.

Not only that, but amazingly – and this could only have happened in the 1960s – Cutler had dossed down in the revolting pigsty two journalist colleagues and I called home in James Street, Rugby. This salubrious thoroughfare has for long been bulldozed out of existence.

It was decided the concert would go ahead, regardless of Jones' death. That Saturday, Chris and I rose early and made our way to Rugby Midland Station, only to find that all the Euston-bound trains were full. Somehow, we managed to convince a guard that our mission was urgent, and he allowed us to ride in the mail carriage. How 1960s is that?

The sky was as blue as our tickets when we joined the crowds heading for Hyde Park. This was the pilgrimage of the baby-boomers, the first generation for more than 50 years not to have been ordered to fight a world war.

There was electricity in the air, an almost indefinable pulse as the tribes of 1960s youth converged on its destination.

The memories are still fresh, even though half a century has passed since that remarkable day. Being in the Press enclosure meant that we were in the company of the emerging rock aristocracy.

And in my case, that meant sitting next to pop starlet Marsha Hunt, a glorious vision in white buckskins, topped off with an Afro-style halo of hair.

At either side of the stage were the courtiers gathered around the throne of his Satanic Majesty himself. Just behind Mick Jagger sat Marianne Faithfull, Julie Felix and the Midlands' own answer to Captain Beefheart, Edgar Broughton.

Sam Cutler hovered close by, ever attentive to his masters' every wish.

Could this be the new alternative government, ready to usher in the Age of Aquarius? Many of us believed it was, a time when the old and corrupt would be swept away on a tide of rock 'n' roll, peace and enlightenment.

There were many minor dramas during the day. I particularly recall the black lad who demonstrated how to 'freak out' and the kindly Hells Angels who may have looked mean, yet behaved in polite contrast to their utterly brutal, murderous American counterparts.

All manner of bands prepared the way for the Stones, most of them now little more than musical memories. Pete Brown's Battered Ornaments, Third

Ear Band, Screw… who knows what became of the musicians that helped to make history on that boiling hot day all those years ago?

A crowd of nearly half a million listened to them in restrained, almost dutiful silence, and then around mid-afternoon, the Stones strode on stage. The footage has been replayed many times – Jagger in Greek soldier's ceremonial 'frock', Richards a living, swaying skull, and new guitarist Mick Taylor looking like a rather bewildered schoolgirl.

They then kicked off their set and were soon hopelessly out of tune, a vision of jaded rebellion that, even then, was showing the first signs of becoming very much part of a new Establishment.

They came and went. As Chris and I filed out of Hyde Park in the dusty heat of that July day, I reflected on the fact that my only sustenance all day had been a hamburger and coke, both bought for what seemed like an extortionate amount.

This had been the first big rock festival – and the rip-off merchants had been more interested in LSD of a different kind.

An hour or so later, we caught the train back to Rugby, suspecting that we had witnessed history in the making. I also dutifully wrote a review of the show which appeared in that week's *Rugby Advertiser*. Well, I'd been given Press tickets, hadn't I? It was only right that I scribbled something.

Mick Jagger and the Stones did indeed become the greatest rock 'n' roll band in the world and Chris Poole ended up working for Jonathan King, a man who went on to become famous for any number of reasons, not all of them good.

As for me, a working lifetime in provincial newspapers lay ahead. But whatever our respective fates, for a magical moment, we had all been united by the common cause of music and idealism once upon a summer's day back in 1969.

That unforgettable concert in Hyde Park basically kick-started the open air rock show culture that has dominated the British summer youth scene for more than half a century.

But before Glastonbury, Knebworth and all the other festivals that were to follow, there was the Rugby one. Yes, you did hear me correctly… there was an open air rock festival held in my home town.

It was staged over three days in a rain-soaked, muddy field on the outskirts of Rugby. Now, this momentous event may not have changed the world, but it was most certainly a pointer to the way things were rapidly changing.

After all these years, I can't recall whose idea it was to hold a large-scale festival in Rugby, but three names spring to mind – Maggie Gibson, Bob Mawby and my colleague Chris Poole.

Maggie was probably the driving force, Bob the fixer, wheeler and dealer, and Chris the man with the all-important contacts.

He knew people working for Blackhill Enterprises, the organisation behind the Stones' Hyde Park gig. Sam Cutler was a leading light with Blackhill, and Chris got to know him quite well. This was how Sam ended up staying in our decaying 'doss' in James Street over the weekend of the festival.

Chris later got a job on the *Eastern Daily Press*, going on to become Jonathan King's press officer. Many years later, King's career would come to an abrupt end as a result of a sex scandal, a sad postscript to the life of a man who had become one of the pop industry's major players during the 1960s, 70s and 80s.

Anyway, I was soon signed up as the festival's Press officer, a new creative departure for me. Looking back, I was probably rather naïve in my general approach and expertise when it came to dealing with the national Press and the top music papers of the day. But there again, I was barely aged 20.

The festival was to be held in a field at Rainsbrook, on the outskirts of Rugby. It's probably now covered with a housing estate. The line-up was incredible, to say the least.

The three days were divided up into three sections – rock, folk and blues. The rock acts featured Pink Floyd, The Nice, Taste and King Crimson among others. In the folk section there were the Strawbs, Bridget St John and Diz Disley, and the blues was represented by artists such as The John Dummer Blues Band, The Groundhogs, The Dave Kelly Blues Band and slide guitar virtuoso Mike Cooper.

By any standards, this was a mind-boggling assembly of the best that the late 1960s had to offer, the crème de la crème of alternative culture.

A few days before the festival in that memorable September, the weather broke. Wouldn't you just know it? Days of clear, blue skies changed to grey, rain-laden clouds that finally burst to bring down torrents of rain.

And as if to anticipate the now-legendary Glastonbury tradition of endless mud, whole sections of the Rainsbrook field became quagmires. Nevertheless, in what would become the standard norm for British festivals, the stage crews soldiered on, the bar and food tents set up… and all the artists themselves duly turned up to perform in their given slot.

I recall having a long and interesting chat with Tony McPhee of the Groundhogs, by then my favourite band other than the Rolling Stones.

Meanwhile, the heavens unloaded their seemingly endless cargoes of rainwater. But the crowd defied it all, erecting makeshift tents or huddled under waterproof gear that miraculously appeared from nowhere.

Of course, I dutifully reported on these three days of music, madness and mud. I faithfully logged the appearances of all the bands and solo artists, including an impressive set by The Big Idea, whose drummer Brian Meredith I had known since my school days at Lawrence Sheriff.

The next edition of the *Advertiser* devoted a whole broadsheet page to my report plus another page of pictures. Gradually and doggedly, rock and pop music culture was starting to get an airing in mainstream media, the old school being forced to understand that this was as newsworthy – or possibly more so – than any court, council or annual general meeting.

Less than four years before, many senior reporters on provincial newspapers such as the *Rugby Advertiser* had regarded pop musicians as merely long-haired layabouts making a racket strumming three chords on a guitar. That's not real music, is it… is it? Well, is it?

But by now, it was clear that rock 'n' roll was here to stay and journalists across the land were starting to realise that they had to reflect this new reality in their papers' columns.

For example, when it emerged that Liverpool chart-topper Billy J Kramer was to marry Rugby girl Ann Ginn at St Mark's Church, Bilton, I was naturally assigned to cover the story.

I was briefed by Editor David Briffett before setting off with photographer John Albyn. He said that if there was a riot by screaming fans, then I was to phone the office immediately and tell Len Archer, who would send out a back-up reporter.

In the event, there were probably more policemen surrounding the church than fans. By the late 1960s, the Mersey sound as personified by Billy J Kramer and the Dakotas was hopelessly out of date, passé, square even.

We were now in the psychedelic era of fuzz tone distortion, 20-minute guitar breaks, drum solos that could last up to half an hour, and songs dominated by unintelligible, surreal 'Dylanesque' lyrics.

Three-minute love songs set to a four-four beat with choppy, twangy rhythm backings were now ancient history, man.

All the same, Billy and his radiant bride were given the new, full *Advertiser* treatment a few days later, once again with a story and picture spread taking up an entire page.

David Briffett personified a new breed of editor who undoubtedly agreed with Bob Dylan that the times were indeed a'changing. The sort of news coverage that was now being implemented by papers such as the *Advertiser* would have been unthinkable only a short while before.

Meanwhile, Len just went along with the flow, and stuck to the things that he understood, the tried and tested.

To be fair, he was a newsman through and through, respected throughout Rugby and very much the public face of the paper. But the climate was now different. Provincial journalism was going through an era of seismic shocks, the vibrations of which are still being felt to this day.

It's time to go north, young man

A FEW weeks after Rugby's free pop music festival, I was thumbing through trade paper the *UK Press Gazette* when I alighted upon a jobs advert for the *Lancashire Evening Post*. It was calling for would-be 'super subs for a super city' to apply.

I had for some time wanted to learn the skills of sub-editing, the art of writing headlines, tightening up or rewriting copy, correcting typographical errors, detecting factual mistakes and designing pages.

The notion of becoming an all-round hack appealed to me. Besides, the sub-editing route could also lead to an editorship, an ambition that would later wane as time went on.

So I applied… and duly got a reply, requesting that I attend an interview at the paper's head office in Fishergate, Preston. This went well, and I was offered a job – but not as a sub-editor, rather as a reporter instead.

Editor Barry Askew told me that the *Post* now had enough sub-editors, but needed more reporters. I accepted… and after more than four years' service, handed in my month's notice at the *Advertiser*.

And so my last week at the paper loomed… along with the biggest story I had yet encountered.

A few days earlier, a young woman had called at the front office and asked to see me about a play she was producing, due to be staged at a local church hall.

It seemed innocuous enough, just the sort of event I had been covering since I'd started back in 1965. However, on the Monday morning of my final week, I received a call from an angry member of the public to report that the 'play' I had mentioned on my page the previous Friday was nothing of the sort.

Whatever this performance purported to be, it had quickly degenerated into an onstage orgy of simulated sex acts, and all conducted in the presence of a group of churchmen and their good lady wives. The sounds of descending jaws heading south must have been deafening.

I immediately told David Briffett and he told me to drop everything and concentrate on getting the full story.

And one by one, I managed to track down the individuals behind the 'play', my first port of call being the woman who had contacted me in the first place.

By the late afternoon of Wednesday, I had my story. It made the front page lead item of that week's *Rugby Advertiser* and must have caused quite a stir across the town. Yes, this may have been the 1960s, but there were still limits.

David Briffett was very pleased with my piece, telling me that I was certainly 'going out with a bang'. And that would have been that, had it not been for a telephone call I received on the Friday night from a *News of the World* reporter.

He wanted to meet me in Rugby that weekend to join him in what was to become a full-blown investigation for a paper that in those days enjoyed a circulation of millions.

This was exactly the kind of story that the *News of the World* wanted. The great British public had always enjoyed the salacious, scandalous and downright grubby sensationalism of the popular Press, and this tale that managed to combine sex and church morals was ideal material for them.

There was just one problem, though. I was due to catch the train to Preston the next day. But after a chat with the man from the 'News of the Screws' I postponed the journey, worked with him on the story, and caught my train late on the Sunday afternoon.

And what an eye-opener of an experience this was for me. Watching his foot-in-the-door techniques, I realised what a cosy, safe little world I had inhabited so far.

Here I was, this big fish in a tiny pond, strutting my stuff, cocksure, haughty, arrogant, full of myself. But I was now hanging out with the really big boys and had begun to realise my limitations.

As a local reporter, I could not afford to offend too many people. A few, yes – but I had to be popular with the majority of readers. This was not the case with our man from the *News of the World*. He could do as he please, write it all down in his notebook… and then disappear back to head office in Fleet Street.

A week later, I was in Preston and working for the *Lancashire Evening Post*. That Sunday, I bought a copy of the *News of the World*, and there was the story headlined: 'Sex shocker of a show in church hall' or something along those lines.

And a few week's later, I received my lineage cheque for around £10, roughly equivalent to half a week's wages. That had certainly been a lucrative few hours' work.

When I look back over the years, that summer of 1969 will always be remembered for any number of momentous events. The death of Rolling Stone Brian Jones, the band's subsequent tribute concert in Hyde Park and the escalating war in Vietnam… these all spring to mind when considering the last year of that memorable decade.

And although it was not quite as important on a world scale, there was another earth-shattering occurrence – for me, at least – that took place in the last few months of the Swinging 60s. And that was when I packed my spotted hanky and moved to Lancashire.

Rugby Clocktower… a time for farewell.

Until then, my only contact with the world above Birmingham had been via *Coronation Street* on the television. I wondered whether everyone would work at t' mill, wear cloth caps and mufflers, and live on a diet of milk stout and hotpot.

That Sunday, the train threaded its way through Stafford, Crewe, Warrington, Wigan and then it was Preston itself. I alighted on to the platform carrying a single brown suitcase and a battered guitar.

If I couldn't be the next Cassandra then perhaps I was destined to be the new Bob Dylan.

I left the station and turned off into Fishergate to find my 'digs' in a cobbled street that had been named after a Crimean War battle. It was Inkerman, Balaclava or Sebastopol Terrace… something like that. Here my memory fails me.

I knocked on the door and met my landlady, predictably dressed in a paisley pinny. She was destined to feed me on an endless diet of meat pies, chips, peas and all drowned in gravy… just the fodder for a growing boy, she would later keep telling me.

I shared with two other lads in a tiny box room that would be my home until I eventually found a flat near the banks of the River Ribble.

Next day, I started work on the *Lancashire Evening Post*. The reporters and sub-editors' offices lay at the top of several flights of stairs, looking out over a sea of roofs and fire escapes.

Editorial departments have traditionally had the worst aspects, for the best views are invariably commandeered by advertising and accounts. It doesn't matter where you go in the country, this was once always the case in the days before the advent of the open plan, out-of-town building that became the norm in the decades that followed.

Anyway, I got into the swing of daily paper work and rapidly acquired the vital skills, many of which are now lost on today's young journalists. These included the ability to compose a story from your notebook while standing in a red telephone box and dictating to copytakers. In those days, evening newspapers published several editions from late morning to mid-afternoon, and so you had to be able to act fast and think on your feet.

Nevertheless, this practice was fraught with dangers. One day, I was covering a murder trial in Lancaster and had been instructed by the news editor to phone copy on the hour.

Unfortunately, my frequent trips to the phone box meant that I missed a crucial part of the case and I got a name wrong. I ended up on the editor's carpet after a complaint was made.

There was a lot going on across Preston in those days and most nights would find me out and about on the town. When not covering council meetings in Fulwood or Penwortham, I could be found enjoying the hospitality of the numerous pubs and hotels, some of which hosted folk clubs. These places were common during the 1960s and provided the perfect opportunity for a lonely lad with a guitar to make friends and maybe create a bit of home-spun music, too.

There were also a number of ex-pat communities in the town and I well remember being invited to a Polish or Czechoslovakian New Year's celebration where the fare seemed to consist solely of ham rolls washed down with pints of mild beer and vodka chasers. How I got out still standing up, I'll never know.

Life could be quite hectic in those days, for a newspaper reporter was expected to work at least two nights a week, and there was also Saturday duty, plus the occasional Sunday shift. In addition, I had joined a folk group called Pennywood, so there were gigs to attend, too.

Our crowning glory was to play at the local Press ball held at the Top Rank dance hall which stood at the top of Fishergate. However, my main preoccupation was covering stories across Lancashire.

I can recall reporting from Blackpool, Fleetwood, Blackburn and almost as far as the Lake District... evening newspapers in those days had much larger circulations than they do today, so all this travelling would result in a very healthy-looking expenses claim every week.

And the people of Lancashire? Well, the older women didn't all wear hairnets and constantly say "'Appen it is" like Ena Sharples, neither did the men sit in the pub snug supping ale with lugubrious faces like *Corrie* stalwart Albert Tatlock.

And nor did the entire population live off a diet of Lancashire hotpot, although I do recall that there were quite a number of pubs that featured this as the main dish on their lunchtime menu.

When the warmer weather arrived, I started to explore my adopted county and discovered that the dark satanic mills cliché was far from true. Riding uphill and down dale on my trusty motorcycle, I discovered the beauty of the Garstang Hills and the verdant countryside around such places as Goosnargh, Grimsargh and Longridge.

However, the jewel in the crown was undoubtedly Southport and its magnificent boulevard, Lord Street. This was the Champs Elysees of the north, the abode of the better-off, as was neighbour Lytham St Annes further along the coast.

Many a sunny weekend was spent relaxing on the dunes and wondering whether the sea would ever come close enough for me to enjoy a paddle.

My time in Lancashire would eventually come to an end and I was ultimately destined to return to my home turf in the Midlands. Nevertheless, my days in the county provided a happy interlude where the people – living up to their fabled reputation – never once failed to extend a warm, northern welcome to a young man who was far from his native heath.

Through the beer glass darkly...

BACK in the days when every town and city would have a centrally placed building that loudly proclaimed this was where the local newspaper resided, you would automatically know the most likely location of the editorial office.

All you had to do was just follow the faint aroma of dust, beer and tobacco smoke and the trail might lead you to a pokey little backroom or attic with head-crunchingly low beams where the only gangway was slightly wider than a person of average build standing sideways.

And all the while trying to avoid the wooden desk splinters that lurked like hidden reefs intent on spearing the first passing object that strayed just that little bit too close.

Each desk would be festooned with clutter of all shapes and sizes, piles of paper, overflowing ashtrays, chipped tea-stained cups, cigarette packets, a stand-up saucy calendar that refused to stand up... and perhaps an empty bottle that had been drained of India Pale Ale the night before.

Non-journalists of a management persuasion would always regard such manifestations of indiscipline with barely concealed disdain, undoubtedly longing for the time when the long-hoped-for tide of uniformity and preferred greyness as personified by the open plan office system would sweep away all the mess in a tsunami of tidiness and absolutely no imagination whatsoever.

But when the walls of this particular Jericho shuddered under the trumpet blasts of change and finally fell, all that happened was that the journalists' preferred chaos merely adapted and moved from shoebox to packing crate before you could say "Hold the front page", which no one has ever said, anyway.

Thankfully, the management dream of Nuremburg rally-style serried ranks of desks never happened. So a new strategy was later devised... if you can't beat 'em, sack 'em.

The Rugby Advertiser building during the 1930s.

What was never understood by the cheap suit brigade was that for the journalist, the office also occasionally doubled up as a home. I've slept on several office floors, washing and shaving in the gents' lavatory when morning came, and then nipping out to a shop to buy a sandwich before that day's work started.

Living in a village meant that it was not always possible to get home after a night job. If the motorcycle or scooter had conked out, had suffered a puncture, the last bus had left, or you were just too tired to make the effort, then a night on the carpet with your rucksack as a pillow was not necessarily all that uncomfortable.

Well, as long as you were young and reasonably fit, that is. I had no age-related aches and pains in those days. Yes, we never realise how lucky we are at the time, do we?

Management never understood the journalistic mentality. They would arrive at bang on nine in the morning and leave at 5.30pm on the dot. Their jobs ended upon leaving the office. Every day of the week, ours just carried on, regardless of the time, where we were, or what we were doing. The job was finished when the job was finished.

There was also occasional criticism of journalists bringing food into the office and eating it at their desks. This was because there was often no time to get out of the office and sit down in a café or park and enjoy a leisurely lunch.

Once, a complaint came down from on high that fish and chips were being eaten in the office – shock, horror – and the smell was bothering the chairman.

The fact that this was the only way that hard-working reporters were going to get any sustenance either didn't occur to the great man or he was just exercising his lordly authority for the hell of it.

A typical example of how reporters would be in the office at all hours of the day and night was the coverage of major agricultural events, such as the Royal Show at Stoneleigh, near Kenilworth, and the British Timken Show that was held every year at Duston, then a village on the outskirts of Northampton.

These huge events might entail a working day of up to 18 hours, because when the show ended, then it was a case of returning to the office to write it all up.

The numbers of class, trophy and cup winners ran into the hundreds. Every one had to be typed up, great care being taken to ensure no mistakes were made. This was no mean feat in itself, because much of this inputting would take place from late evening to the early hours when brains were becoming decidedly weary.

All this took place after you had travelled back to Rugby in the office van feeling tired, hungry, sweaty after a day in the broiling sun, and with the stale taste of that day's cigarettes and beer in your mouth.

You would have been wearing a jacket all the time, too. In those days, men seemed to wear this item of clothing regardless of the prevailing weather conditions, plus the obligatory collar and tie.

It could be blazing sunshine but it made no difference whatsoever. When meeting the public, you had to look neat and tidy because it was expected of you. There was no such concept as casual.

Comfort didn't come into it. And as for a cooling, rejuvenating shower… these didn't exist in most homes. It was a couple of baths a week and that would have to suffice.

That long day covering a show might only finally end at three or four in the morning. But regardless of when you eventually hit the sheets, there was still no time for a lie-in as far as I was concerned. Being the youngest, I had been assigned another task to perform.

British Timken was held on a Saturday and pre-ordered copy had to be sent to the *Leicester Mercury* the next day. And by post, too – there was obviously no convenient internet back then to make things just that little bit easier.

This huge wedge of typewritten copy paper could not be phoned over in the usual way, which is why it had to be dropped into the letterbox at Rugby's head post office in North Street in time for it to reach the *Leicester Mercury* by Monday morning.

The major agricultural shows entailed some very hard work indeed. But by flogging the story to a top-selling evening paper meant that it was possible to make quite a bit of cash from all that labour. You were, after all, paid by the column line of printed text, and there would be very many of those in a show report.

But to this day, I cannot bear to visit an agricultural show, even though now it would be purely as a spectator. I have too many memories of the ordeal they could be all those years ago.

Newspapers have changed out of all recognition over the last 50 years. Circulations are but a shadow of what they had once been and staff levels slashed to the bare minimum needed to get the papers out.

Many were once family-owned. Now, ownerships have contracted into a handful of enormous, anonymous companies. And the internet has become the master rather than the servant of once great publications.

Everything has been turned upon its head. Once, reporters were expected to be out and about, searching for stories. Nowadays, they are virtually desk-bound, required to process the endless press releases that now form the bulk of printed, radio and television news.

Not so long ago, journalists were walking the streets, calling in at post office, pub, rectory and railway station to see what was happening on their patch.

Notice boards were studied with keen eyes, peeled, probing and picking, looking for that badly-written announcement that might be the germ of the biggest story so far encountered. The off-diary tale was king.

Editors are no longer in charge of just one publication, they must preside over many. Mistakes are therefore legion, sometimes ending in hearings at which the presiding adjudicator might ask whether the editor reads all the copy that goes into his papers.

As if. How could any human being be capable of seeing every single word printed in six or seven papers that constantly appear on the news stands throughout a circulation area of many square miles?

But not infrequently, an editor is called to task over a serious error of fact, a piece of operational misjudgement, or hauled before professional inquisitors over a columnist some local tedious windbag, politician or bigwig feels has gone too far.

How could one person ever be accountable for so much in working conditions as absurd as these? This is cloud cuckoo land to be sure.

Many, but not all, editors these days are company stooges through and through. The modern newspaper company is packed to the gunwales with unquestioning individuals who have to be 'on message' with boardroom strategy and thinking.

They are now selling 'product'. It might as well be baked beans, light bulbs, cotton buds or tomato sauce. Editorial executives have for long been sent on management courses at which they rub shoulders with supermarket managers, building society counter staff, and a hundred and one other unrelated callings.

And after a day learning the jargon, ham psychology, staff motivation techniques and all the rest of the corporate mumbo-jumbo, the journalist will retire to the bar in the evening to be bored rigid in the company of people with whom he or she has nothing in common.

Product, product... and more product. And when that product goes into decline, as it most surely will, the editor will follow his masters' instructions and be obliged to sack his fellow journalists.

For a few, this will all eventually prove to be too much... and they will do the honourable thing and leave provincial journalism altogether for the more verdant pastures of press relations and lucrative consultancy positions.

But there is one key factor why papers are in freefall. And that's down to the utter foolhardiness of the universally adopted editorial policy of uploading every single news item to the internet where the public can read it for free.

Journalists are told that there is no other way, old media cannot stand still, it must move with the times. But it is testimony to the sheep-like stupidity of modern management that, instead of harnessing a resource and making it complement the existing media, bosses have not only singularly failed, but also ruined entire enterprises in the process.

The greed of shareholders is also a factor. There's nothing wrong with investing in a company – millions of us do it – but people who put their money into newspapers have totally unrealistic expectations.

Shareholders want more and more growth on their annual dividends. They put pressure on managements to achieve this, which in turn means that it's the man or woman on the editorial floor who must pay the price...

This isn't meant to be a treatise against capitalism. It's merely a statement of plain fact regarding the state of the modern newspaper industry. For despite what some of the more morally superior among us may fondly imagine, we're all capitalists in one way or another.

There is a depressing inevitability about all this, which is probably the reason why many youngsters leaving pre-entry training courses no longer view newspapers as being a viable, long-term career prospect.

Time and again, those of us who read online sites that cover provincial journalism issues wonder at how they can seemingly create the impression that local newspapers represent some kind of future.

Editors have been leaving the industry in droves over the last few years. This is routinely portrayed as 'moving on to pastures new' or merely another step upwards in a glittering career... when the bitter truth is that the person concerned has been sacked, made redundant, forced out because it's all just too stressful, or their post absorbed by another faceless person in a cheap suit.

And the blame for this exodus can be laid at the feet of one, all-powerful grouping. Meet the Number Crunchers... you may not know them at the moment, but by God you soon will.

They all sing from the same hymn sheet, the most popular being the one that goes to the tune of *Let's Blame the Internet for Everything*. Despite the fact that newspapers coped with the advent of radio in the 1930s, television in the 1950s, and actually increased their circulations despite all, for some reason the latest technology is ruining it for everyone.

It's not us, Guv. Someone else is to blame. Perhaps we're all to blame.

The internet is no more than just another competitor, to be lived with or seen off if necessary as the older technology adapts. This reasoning is, of course, lost on the modern newspaper manager. Why? Because most of them are stupid, grey little people, that's why.

And yet... there are a few survivors not lost in this maelstrom of mediocrity. There are still a few family-owned papers that have blended the old and new technologies to make a success of their businesses. And the runaway success of the *Metro* has surely been proof that newspapers still have a role.

Bright layout, good use of colour, and bite-size stories that can be read on a single train journey should have been a pointer for everyone else. The *Metro* management obviously identified their target audience, and acted accordingly. And good for them. It worked.

Instead, the rest just ploughed a shrinking furrow with template design, stories being fed straight into text boxes by reporters, a total absence of sub-editorial judgement, and a growing reliance on badly taken crazily photo-shopped photographs submitted by members of the public.

I vividly remember challenging an editor during the latter days of my career as a staff journalist. Creating an imaginary scenario, I suggested to him that if I asked my bank manager for a loan to set up a new business that would give everything away free, this person would probably laugh in my face and then show me the door.

It made no difference. He was toeing the company line and even though there were no plans to install a pay wall, everything had to go online because it was "The coming thing".

Very Nuremberg, that… just following orders then. 'Coming thing' may be mindless but we stick to policy because… well, it's the 'coming thing', isn't it?

And it was all rather prophetic, because 'the coming thing' would actually not only eventually herald my own demise, but also that of quite a few of my colleagues.

The vast majority of newspaper executives have traditionally been recruited from advertising and accounts departments. These people have historically always regarded the journalists as being a costly inconvenience, which is why they had no qualms about making thousands of us redundant when the first opportunities arose.

Don't blame us, could be their mantra. Blame the internet. The fact that it was always – and forever will be – good journalism that makes people want to read newspapers escapes them.

As far as I'm concerned, it's an undeniable truth that newspaper managements are solely to blame for the industry's decline. Meanwhile, the British public have gradually forsaken what to them is an inferior product, and chosen to get their news from the numerous electronic devices that now flood the marketplace.

Managements like to pretend that they have thousands of readers 'in print and online'. But how much revenue is coming in if there is no pay wall? If you had the choice between coughing up the cash, or getting something for nothing, what would you do?

The tragedy is that had there been proper investment in quality journalism which would have protected the older media, while working in partnership with the internet, this careers wasteland might still be the verdant acres it most surely once was.

Little wonder then that the modern newspaper editor can't get his or her head around the problem.

Hopefully, there will always be room for the professionally-driven, community-minded local journalist. But the sad facts of the matter are that there will just be fewer of them.

And then – and perhaps only then – the politicians will suddenly wake up to the reality that all this catastrophic loss of journalistic scrutiny endangers the future of democracy.

They will then make brave speeches in the House of Commons, talk at Rotary Club dinners, and generally say how awful it all is. But like politicians throughout history, they will come up with no solutions.

And even if they did, it would all be far, far too late. The stable door has been open for far too long and the horses now well and truly bolted.

Yet despite my sadness about what has happened to an industry that somehow managed to sustain me all my working life, I look back down the years and often smile to myself.

I enjoy the occasional reunion with old colleagues – always in a pub, of course – and we will talk about the old days as old men always do, maybe glossing over the hard times and telling tall tales of the characters we knew once upon a working lifetime ago.

And finally, after several hours of beery banter, my old comrade-in-arms and I will bid farewell and part company, both of us making our ways back home and thinking about how it was all those years ago.

As for me, my thoughts will inevitably turn to that hot July day back in 1965 when I entered the reporters' office at the *Rugby Advertiser*... and life would never be the same again.

Raise your glasses to absent friends

MANY of the people mentioned in this story have passed on. I use this common expression because I've always felt that the word 'died' is so final. Which it is, of course... to some extent, anyway.

However, if you feel the end of physical existence really does mean farewell to everyone and everything, and all that's left is a bleak Eternity of oblivion, then that may be all right with you. But it's not good enough for me, if you don't mind. It's just too... well, final, as I said.

The reason I say this is because the people I have written about in this book were, in the main, larger-than-life characters, the like of which we will never see again.

And it's because of this that they will remain immortal... in my memory at least.

Len Archer, for all his faults, was a consummate newspaperman. David Briffett, John Hardeman, David Berry, Ted Pincham, Guy Edgson too... I would like to think that they are all now having a drink together in some celestial bar where the towels never go up, the bell doesn't ring, and the ever-smiling barmaids are all fair and buxom.

Perhaps even John Hardeman won't mind sharing the Big Man's table for a change with former adversary David Berry.

And then there's Geoff Ambler. Perhaps, because of my youth, I misunderstood him all those years ago, maybe he did have my best interests at heart after all... but I doubt very much whether any further light will be shed on this.

All I know is that I have tried to be fair to these people and would like to think that my reminiscences are accurate and faithful recollections of the individuals concerned.

And if I have offended anyone, then the best I can do is offer a conditional apology. Conditional? Yes. Because I've honestly told it how it was, working on a provincial newspaper just as the 1960s were about to take off and leave the runway.

Not only that, but I feel I've related the course of events to the best of my abilities. The devil was always in the detail... the printer's devil, at least.

It's also true to say that there were many happy times but also dark periods when I could have easily given it all up and plumped for a less frenetic calling. But that would have been boring. And 'boring' is something that has never interested me.

And while it's perfectly true that while I may like this idea of the celestial bar that never shuts, and the rock 'n' roll gig with the permanent encore, all the available evidence suggests that life is still for the living, something I intend to do – God willing, of course – as long as possible.

You see, I'm not quite ready to meet my old muckers just yet. Heaven will have to wait a little while longer, I'm afraid.

The End